Joseph Randolph Bowers

Sacred Teachings from the Mi'kmaq Medicine Lodge

Rev Dr Joseph Randolph Bowers

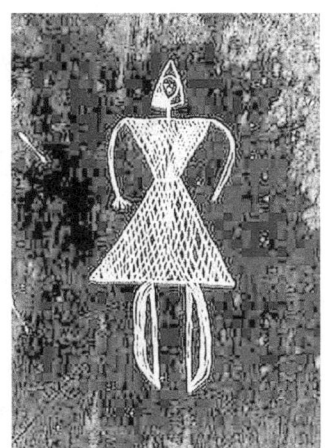

Second Edition

St Clare Cottage

Sacred Teachings

Publication

Sacred Teachings from the Mi'kmaq Medicine Lodge Copyright © 2023 Joseph Randolph Bowers, all rights reserved. All rights reserved. No part of this publication may be reproduced or transmitted in any form or by any means, electronic or mechanical, including photocopying, recording, or by any information retrieval and storage system, without prior written permission of the publisher. St Clare Cottage, an Imprint of Ability Therapy Specialists Pty Ltd, PO Box 4065, Armidale, New South Wales, Australia 2350. First published during 2013, under the title Sacred Teachings from the Medicine Lodge, the first edition was a Limited Release and is permanently out of print.

ISBN: 978-1-925034-21-9 (Paperback) Second Edition

Keywords: Mi'kmaq, Spirituality, Culture, Ceremony, Meditation, Ecology, First Nation, Canadian, Native American, Personal Growth, Shamanism

Disclaimer: This book is produced as a personal reflective tool only, to assist readers in personal development, and is not an authoritative source of information. Readers ought to seek direct medical advice as your authoritative source of information. The publisher disclaims all liability for all claims, expenses, losses, damages and costs any person may incur as a result of the information contained in this publication, for any reason, being inaccurate, or incomplete in any way or incapable or achieving any purpose. These statements do not disclaim statutory obligations as deemed necessary under the law.

Joseph Randolph Bowers

About this Book

A rare window into the often mysterious, sacred, and hidden world of First Nation, Native Canadian, and North American Indian culture and spiritual teachings. Arising from Ancient Springs. First published by the Mi'kmaq community in a regional periodical, and later carefully adapted for a wider audience. Now in Second Edition. *Sacred Teachings from the Mi'kmaq Medicine Lodge* is a Sacred Medicine Bundle rich in traditional teachings and contemporary reflections. Based on the mystical teachings of the age-old seasonal moon cycles, the Sacred Circle of Readings provides a Liturgy of Creation around the major traditional Ceremonies. A source of great wealth and power in spirituality, wisdom, and psychosocial healing. Readers will be given heart. Indian spirituality comes alive. New pathways open up. A way forward appears through living a more sacred, balanced, and honourable life.

About the Author

Hon Rev Dr Joseph Randolph Bowers is a scholar in spirituality, counselling, and health. Dr Bowers an Associate Scholar with the Centre for World Indigenous Studies, and a member of Spiritual Directors International. Dr Bowers is an Honorary of the Australian Counselling Association, co-founder of the Australian Counselling Research Journal. He is among the founders of the Psychotherapy and Counselling Federation of Australia. Dr Bowers works in private practice as a Senior Clinical Behaviour Specialist Counsellor Psychotherapist. Rev Dr Bowers is a Registered Marriage Celebrant and founder of the Eremitas Familia Minima, the Minims. Dr Bowers is author of over 250 works including, *The Practice of Counselling*; *Sacred Teachings from the Medicine Lodge*; *On the Threshold: Personal Transformation and Spiritual Awakening*; *Mi'kmaq Puoinaq Two Spirit Medicine*; *Homophobia and Healing: Psychotherapy and the Psychology of Prejudice*; *Mass of Creation: Liturgies and Prayers for all Occasions;* and *Solitude Awakens: The Heart Forest Mountain Way.*

Joseph Randolph Bowers

In loving memory

Virginia Jane 'Jenny' (Doucette) Bernard
December 30, 1963 - November 27, 2012
Eskasoni First Nation

Daughter of Georgina (Denny) Doucette and Noel Doucette. Sister of Vaughan, Mike, Noel Jr., Daniel, Donald, Bernice, Ruby and John. Wife of John Joseph Bernard. Mother of Theresa, Caroline, Jenny, Allister, and Olivia. Grand Mother of John David, Jorja Rayne, Christopher, Wyatt, Kaylynn, Marshall Jr., John Andrew, Precious and Richard. You are the Star who Sings. You Sing with Your Light.

Acknowledgements

This work was first published in the "Eagle Medicine Column" by the Mi'kmaq Maliseet Nations News, Volume 18-20, 2007-2009. Many thanks go to Wanda Meuse, then Editor in Chief of the Mi'kmaq Maliseet Nations News, whose support and kindness will always be remembered with great fondness. A second Publication occurred under "The Collected Eagle Medicine Column" by Cape Breton University Mi'kmaq Resource Centre Special Collection, 2009. Thank you from the heart to Diane Chisholm of the Cape Breton University Mi'kmaq Resource Centre (MRC) for her assistance and friendship over the years, and to the then MRC Director Patrick Johnson for being of good heart and welcoming my work within the highly esteemed Resource Centre.

Highest of regards are extended to Annette LeBlanc-Power whose life-long friendship has meant so much to me. You have truly been my Morning Star. Thank you for encouraging me to write for the Mi'kmaq Maliseet press, your energy of love is now manifest in this book. Blessings and wela'lia to Dwayne Andrew Wannamarra Kennedy for your constant friendship and unconditional love. Wela'lia for helping me to reconnect with my People, and for opening many doors by visiting Mi'kma'ki with me during 2005, and for your patience during the long hours of work and writing. Blessings to the Kennedy family, especially the late Elder Austin John; and Elder Rosamond Grace Kennedy, and all of your children; Denny and Donna, Denis and Lisa, David and Kay, Jonna and Chris, and all the grandchildren and great grandchildren. Many blessings to Elder Auntie Diane Roberts, for seeing and offering hope and a pathway home to reconnect with Mi'kmaq family.

Spiritual blessings to family in Mi'kma'ki, including mother Jeanette; Angela, Betty and Charlie, and their families, children and grandchildren; and to all of our cousins and relations near and far. Especially, Chief Frank Meuse, Wanda Finigan, and Rose Meuse of Bear River First Nation; James Joseph Jeremy of Acadia First Nation, Wildcat. Blessings to Georgina Doucette, of Eskasoni First Nation, and to your children, my brothers and sisters, who we love so dearly. Especially Jenny, whose love and friendship moved me so much and changed my life. This book is in her memory. To sisters Bernice and Ruby with endless love. Many blessings to Ellen Hunt, your love and friendship means the world to me. To CatherineAnn and Mac Fuller, your kindness and love have opened many doors.

To Kisiku'skw Paqtism, for awakening in this generation, a new Seventh Generation, and the fourteenth of our line since the marriage of two families during 1652. You awaken the White Buffalo Calf Women who has again walked through the Eastern Door into our Nation. You offer these Sacred Teachings. We are wise to listen. As the Elder Grandmothers have taught us, we dedicate our lives to Your work. To the People of the Mi'kmaq Nation near and far, blessings and strength in your spirit. My humble life across the planet is witness to the fact of our resilience and hope. Heartfelt thanks for welcoming these teachings within your local press, and for welcome us whenever we have visited and stayed for a time in your beautiful homes and communities. Thank you for encouraging and giving me the 'gentle push' to continue on this path and to give back this work to our people. Wela'lia. M'sit No'koma. Ta'ho.

Sacred Teachings

Table of Contents

PUBLICATION 2

ABOUT THIS BOOK 3

ABOUT THE AUTHOR 4

IN LOVING MEMORY 5

ACKNOWLEDGEMENTS 6

TABLE OF CONTENTS 8

INTRODUCTION 12
    SPIRITUALITY MAKING MEANING IN LIFE 18
    THE INDIGENOUS SCIENCES 19
    CULTURAL RESPECT 24
    THE WIGWAM OF THE PEOPLE 30
    HOW TO ENJOY THIS COLLECTION 39
    CONCLUSION 48

THE FIRST MOON CYCLE: YEAR ONE 52

KESIK/WINTER MOONS 53
    JANUARY PUNAMUJUIKU'S FROST FISH MOON 53
        Reflection 61
    FEBRUARY APIKNAJIT SNOW BLINDER MOON 63
        Reflection 71
    MARCH SIWKEWIKU'S SPAWNING MOON 73
        Reflection 79

SIWKW/SPRING MOONS 80

APRIL PENATEMUIKU'S EGG LAYING MOON 80
Reflection 83
MAY ETQOLJEWIKU'S FROG-CROAKING MOON 84
Reflection 88
JUNE NIPNIKU'S SUMMER MOON 89
Reflection 93

NIPK/SUMMER MOONS 94

JULY PESKEWIKU'S FEATHER-SHEDDING MOON 94
Reflection 99
AUGUST PESKEWIKU'S FEATHER-SHEDDING MOON 101
Reflection 105
SEPTEMBER WIKUMKEWIKU'S MOOSE-CALLING MOON 106
Reflection 109

TOQA'Q/AUTUMN MOONS 112

OCTOBER WIKEWIKU'S ANIMAL-FATTENING MOON 112
Reflection 117
NOVEMBER KEPTEKEWIKU'S RIVER-FREEZING MOON 119
Reflection 123
DECEMBER KJIKU'S THE GREAT MOON 124
Reflection 129

THE SECOND MOON CYCLE: YEAR TWO 132

KESIK/WINTER MOONS 133

JANUARY PUNAMUJUIKU'S FROST FISH MOON 133
Reflection 135
FEBRUARY APIKNAJIT SNOW BLINDER MOON 137
Reflection 139
MARCH SIWKEWIKU'S SPAWNING MOON 143
Reflection 145

SIWKW/SPRING MOONS 147

APRIL PENATEMUIKU'S EGG LAYING MOON 147

Reflection *149*
MAY ETQOLJEWIKU'S FROG-CROAKING MOON 152
   Reflection *154*
JUNE NIPNIKU'S SUMMER MOON 157
   Reflection *159*

NIPK/SUMMER MOONS 162

JULY PESKEWIKU'S FEATHER-SHEDDING MOON 162
   Reflection *164*
AUGUST KISIKWEKEWIKU'S FRUIT AND BERRY-RIPENING MOON 166
   Reflection *168*
SEPTEMBER WIKUMKEWIKU'S MOOSE-CALLING MOON 169
   Reflection *171*

TOQA'Q/AUTUMN MOONS 173

OCTOBER WIKEWIKU'S ANIMAL-FATTENING MOON 173
   Reflection *175*
NOVEMBER KEPTEKEWIKU'S RIVER-FREEZING MOON.......................... 176
   Reflection *178*
DECEMBER KJIKU'S THE GREAT MOON 179
   Reflection *181*

THE THIRD MOON CYCLE: YEAR THREE 182

KESIK/WINTER MOONS 183

JANUARY PUNAMUJUIKU'S FROST FISH MOON 183
   Reflection *185*
FEBRUARY APIKNAJIT SNOW BLINDER MOON 186
   Reflection *188*
MARCH SIWKEWIKU'S SPAWNING MOON 191
   Reflection *193*

SIWKW/SPRING MOONS 195

APRIL PENATEMUIKU'S EGG LAYING MOON 195
   Reflection *197*
MAY ETQOLJEWIKU'S FROG-CROAKING MOON 201
   Reflection *203*

June Nipniku's Summer Moon 207
   Reflection *209*

NIPK/SUMMER MOONS 210

July Peskewiku's Feather-shedding Moon 210
   Reflection *212*
August Kisikwekewiku's Fruit and Berry-ripening Moon 213
   Reflection *215*
September Wikumkewiku's Moose-calling Moon 217
   Reflection *219*

TOQA'Q/AUTUMN MOONS 221

October Wikewiku's Animal-fattening Moon 221
   Reflection *223*
November Keptekewiku's River-freezing Moon 224
   Reflection *226*
December Kjiku's The Great Moon 229
   Reflection *231*

POSTSCRIPT 2013 233

POSTSCRIPT 2023 240

Introduction

Pjila'si ~ Welcome, come in, sit down. This greeting speaks from the heart. Pjila'si means an offering of hospitality. In traditional culture the word is used to invite a guest into a community and into the place of family, the Wigwam, or what others call the Tipi. To be invited into this space around the 'fire' within the heart of family represents openness among the Native People towards developing a relationship that is based in trust, honour and respect.

This writing will also invite respect and a sense of the Sacred. For this reason, I will capitalise certain words like 'People' when the feeling moves me to suggest a sense of the Sacred. This is why at other times I might use the same word but do not always use capitalisation. In the traditional way, all of life is Sacred and all of life is Ceremony. To bring this awareness forward I will use simple tools in the English language to suggest a different way of perceiving.

The Mi'kmaq Nation is located on the North Eastern coast of North America and stretches from what is now called Newfoundland, south to the New England State of Maine, including the provinces of Nova Scotia, New Brunswick, Prince Edward Island, and west including the Eastern tundra region of Quebec. The Mi'kmaq Nation is governed by a system of democracy sustained for hundreds and thousands of years through elected Chiefs and honoured Elders. Regional Chiefs gathered to share across tribal boundaries, and across the Mi'kmaw territory a common understanding of trade, commerce, law and justice was entertained and respected. International diplomacy was well known and highly regarded, as many travelled far and wide, trading and learning the customs of other nations. An extensive Inter-national Wabanaki Confederacy existed for hundreds of years prior to colonisation of the territories by Europeans.

If you look closely, I have added in English after the word Pjila'si a triad of meanings. In a sense, in this book Pjila'si as a word itself represents the Eastern Door of the Wigwam where the First and Sacred Pole of the structure is dug into Mother Earth. This is the Passageway between the Worlds. The word itself symbolises a personal spiritual or conscious change. By entering this space of ceremony and respect, you risk entering the Sacred Country of our Ancestors.

The additional three meanings represent the other Cardinal Directions of South, West and North. These meanings suggest the spirit and feeling of the word over the years. Most words in Mi'kmaw hold many associations, meanings and stories. The words are given life by the People. Even while my knowledge of the language could be improved and it pains me to feel this grief and loss for our language, I know in heart that the Mi'kmaw language holds the sacred feeling of respect we carry today for all of creation. The language embodies our spirituality, identity, culture and our sense of ethics, morality, and justice. The language expresses our esteem for knowledge and wisdom and has inspired and sustained our extensive history of science and exploration including our ancient practice of charting the stars and reading their meaning in culture, world events and familial life. Our language is deeply meaningful, as suggested by ancient stone petroglyphs and our written hieroglyphic text.

Pjila'si means 'Welcome.' This word exists in many languages around the world and expresses open arms and hands of greeting, acceptance of others as they are, and an invitation into a cultural space of sharing.

Pjila'si means 'Come in.' This phrase also arises in cultures around the world and suggests that a person enter into a place and space that is defined as unique to a family. To enter the space of family means that you become engaged in the life of that family. You are no longer 'outside' and cannot be considered an 'outsider.' To 'come in' means to physically enter into a different place. This suggests that one must make a personal change. The physical act of entry requires openness to listen, dialogue, and to pay respect to the family home and the people who live there. In the actual space of the Wigwam, a person must physically bend or bow forward and then step over the base-threshold of the Wigwam, over which the door flap hangs to keep out the cold and to prevent rain from entering. The importance of this act of physically bending low to enter a Wigwam holds great significance. How a person holds their body while entering shows much about the individual's disposition and character.

Coming into this intimate space of the family, one needs to adjust your eyes to see in a different way, in a world that is illuminated by a Family Fire around which the People sit. You are asked to take your place, usually a place of honour held in great respect by the family. Here you are not only invited to participate but also to pay respect to the members of the family, even while you might take time to learn the customs and manners of those sitting around the fire.

Our late father, Joe, always welcomed people into the wigwam of the home with a bear hug. He felt it a joyful obligation to show this deep respect for visitors. He welcomed them into his heart. Over the years we learned so much from observing this custom. Many people were clearly not comfortable getting a big hug. But regardless who came through the door, they must have sensed that this was part of the culture and custom, and they respected Dad enough to allow him to make this gesture a genuine show of mutual respect.

Reflecting on this experience it is easy to see that in traditional cultures certain customs and ceremonies are maintained to keep a higher level of respect and care for people's well-being. An innate wisdom guided these decisions and people today are searching for these basic approaches to life to bring back meaning, identity and purpose to our lives. We have this power within us to influence our interactions with others. We can decide how we will greet one another, and how we will treat one another. To deny this basic human right that exists within each of us would be like refusing to acknowledge that we have skin on our bodies. In this way, 'come in' is a layer of meaning that reminds me of my father's warmth and courtesy in welcoming friends and strangers into our home.

Pjila'si also means an invitation to 'sit with us,' and this again suggests an even deeper meaning. In the traditional Wigwam, everyone in the Lodge of the Family sits with humility upon Mother Earth. You too are invited to take your place of honour among the People. By inviting you into this place to sit, you are participating in the ancient customs of a People whose traditions go back hundreds of thousands of years to the dawn of time. Sitting in this way is more than merely social. Sitting in this sense is an opening of the self by connecting with the energy of Mother Earth, as we sit upon Her with only dried grass, animal skins and blankets. Sitting in this way around the Family Fire is a spiritual experience of opening to Listening, to Being Real to Your True Self, and to sharing in the Sacred Everyday Life of the Old Ones of the People.

In our family, inviting people into the home involved a warm embrace by the door or in the living room or kitchen, and very often cups of tea or coffee, an offer of something to eat, and in the midst of this an offer of a place to sit, whether at the table in the kitchen or on a comfy chair in the living room. Many of these basic customs of welcoming, greeting, embracing and sharing endure to this day in families across most countries around the world. In the Mi'kmaw Way, welcoming, greeting, embracing and sharing from the Four Sacred Directions that provide basic human respect. These may be expressed in many different ways, but we can agree that these customs arise from ancient cultural practices and are not exclusive to any one culture.

There is one more meaning of the invitation to 'sit down' that comes to mind now. In today's world people are forgetting to spend quality time with each other. Television, mobile phones, hand-held devices, and many distractions are preventing people from seeing what is in front of them. We are social and familial creatures. We need each other. We become lost emotionally and psychologically when quality time with others is compromised over long periods of time. We lose social skills in relating to our inner world and to others. When our focus is on technology, our humanity can become lost.

The meaning of sitting with others in all traditional cultures was about being real, transparent, and accessible. The approach is to be direct, open of heart, and willing to listen, and then to share from your own thoughts and feelings. The art of conversation was a part of everyday life, and people could not survive socially without having these basic skills. Today people can survive on their own without much direct conversation or communication. We text one another on phones, but spend less time talking with each other face to face. While self-reliance is a great blessing in many ways, over the years people feel empty and like they have lost something they find difficult to articulate. I'm sure part of this loss comes from the loneliness we feel in modern day living, when our quality time of sitting with each other has become so rare. When we find ourselves in social situations many people will feel awkward and unable to cope with direct human communication.

There is also a spiritual meaning to these teachings about welcoming, greeting, embracing and sharing. While we respect that every reader will have a different set of beliefs and values, we will also be honest and open with you about our beliefs and values. Take what you need and let go of the rest. Don't take my statements as a gospel truth, as this is not our intention at all. We live in a cultural world where people have extremely different beliefs and values. In truth, it has always been this way.

In the Old Days of the People we may have held more commonly held beliefs, values and practices. We call this cultural cohesion. But even when there is a society that shares common values, there are always many people who are very creative and stand outside of the basic assumptions. Every person is their own person. In traditional culture, we celebrate and encourage individuality even while we know that our identity exists because of our family, tribe and nation. We grow up learning to pay respect where respect is due. We watch our Elders to see what their conduct is like. If they live respect for others, Elders gain much greater respect themselves. An "Elder" is not an older person, but a being who has attained a high degree of loving kindness, humility, patience, creativity, capacity for enduring suffering, and a form of wisdom that can only grow from real life experience.

Spirituality Making Meaning in Life

In the same way, when I say 'spiritual' or 'spirituality' my meaning to these words might take me several books to explain the richness and depth of these words. Today these words are taboo in mainstream cultures as well as in many Native cultures. One of my cousins told me once that they had no spirituality. They did not believe in a spiritual reality. Their world was made up of simple decisions to improve their life. They did work personally to improve their circumstances and to work on their personality. And that was their sense of values.

When reflecting on these ideas, on one hand my cousin made a lot of sense. Ironically, by taking a strong stand toward basic values that express the modern era's material and empirical philosophy, my kin described what our scholarly analysis suggests is a form of spirituality. In this classic academic sense, a spirituality is simply how people make their sense of meaning. As such, an atheist has a spirituality. Likewise, the word 'spiritual' at its roots means 'expressing the spirit or energy of life.' When we strip away the trappings of religion, theology, and even cultural traditions, we find a basic landscape that everyone shares. A common humanity. A form of life that is rendered sacred only because we decide to treat each other with respect and human kindness.

Mi'kmaw spiritual teachings suggest that spirituality is a way of life. But what do the Elders really mean when they say that all of life is ceremony, and all ceremony is life? I suggest they mean that when we slow down enough to observe real life all around us and within us, we will find the most basic structure of life is full of meaning. Full stop. Period. End of the theology lesson. In Native Ways, the rest is up to you. You are not forced to then believe in any particular approach to life - but you will be held accountable for your actions from a place of fairness, justice, and within high standards of showing regard for others.

Otherwise, all Native spirituality is based on observations of the world around us. The insight that you come to have relies on your personal experiences of life. Where have you walked? Who have you met? What have you seen and heard? What meanings have you attached to these experiences? These become your Sacred Story. We say, 'our Stories are our Medicine.' This is our spiritual and cultural Way.

The Indigenous Sciences

For these reasons we see Mi'kmaw culture and spirituality as extremely in sync with modern science and scholarship. The practice of observing life and learning by testing, making mistakes, coming to terms with reality, and basing one's beliefs on lived experience is a basic and integral scientific method. This form of Indigenous Science is age old and part of our ancient and contemporary traditions. The cultural maps of the world, how Mi'kmaq people experienced the world and made meaning of that world, are infinitely practical and spiritual in their elegance and integral simplicity.

For example, Mi'kmaq people like most people around the world have had many experiences of their family members becoming ill and passing over into another realm of existence. It was felt that this other realm existed because people experienced their loved one's energy returning after the death of the body to communicate a message. Elders of high degree took vision quests and visited the World of Spirits, and it became known that different Worlds exist where Spirits live lives similar to us who dwell in the Earth World. The Milky Way became associated with the ultimate Dwelling Place of the Ancestors. To that Place we return when our journey is finished, and we are ready to re-join the Original Teachings. Even then, our journey may begin again. And many Mi'kmaq observe that the spirit or energy of certain family members returns again to live among the People, born in a new infant or living within the skin-time of an animal, bird or other creature.

You may well discount these beliefs as nonsense and superstition. You may also wonder how we have accepted these beliefs at face value, given my decades of training and working in the academe of many western universities. But we suggest, if a person discounts out of hand another person's observations and beliefs formed from their lived experience, that individual possesses very little wisdom and shows even less respect.

In many years of education and training in the classical western arts and sciences, our basic approach relies on listening and respecting people's beliefs and values. From this stance we can entertain any and all belief systems. In this mindset of openness, life is profoundly enriching. Beliefs are like metaphors of meaning - they do not lead to think in absolute terms but more like a poet, musician or painter whose art expresses the infinite wonder of the universe around us. We do not have to define everything. We can rather enjoy exploring the world. And when we have made a hard and fast belief, life tends to throw a challenging experience that questions the belief and gives rise to new understanding.

For example, we never grew up believing in the transmission of a person's spirit across different lifetimes. Many cultures call this reincarnation. In Mi'kmaw tradition, there is debate on this point, and many ancient stories suggest the fluidity and learning path of the spirit or being who comes to inhabit the body. If there is a clear teaching around the transmigration of soul, the Mi'kmaw approach may be around the emphasis on an evolution of awareness within creation. There are many suggestions of how our Ancestors observed the nature of the human person, their energetic presence, their spirit, and how that energy took on different shapes, faces, skins, and seemed to translate into different lifetimes. In my understanding of Mi'kmaw philosophy and cosmology, this suggests a much more complex notion that goes far beyond simple explanations of reincarnation.

But there again, Native spirituality tends to complex and layered and has not so far been reduced to a theology, doctrine, or dogma. These realities may change over the next several generations as our People interact and react to the many challenges of cultural relations with the other tribes and systems of humanity on Turtle Island and beyond. But as to Native spirituality becoming a religion, that seems unlikely and is hard to say. We observe this even while our path has moved us toward being an ordained minister and traditional Pipe Carrier and Keeper of Medicine; and we note that the readings in this book over the years have come to be used as sacred texts within the Mass of Creation.

In traditional cosmology our spirits are inter-related to all beings, while at the same time possessing many unique and varied powers that allow us to shape-shift and to manifest different qualities, characteristics, appearances and values. Many people in everyday life have described very old memories, as if they had lived before. We have the common saying of a child being an old soul. Children often speak knowledge, observations and memories that they could not possibly possess without a spiritual level of existence. Many in the community also acknowledge openly that a child is the embodiment of a sister, brother, auntie or uncle who passed over years before. But in any case, my Christian upbringing did not include the idea of reincarnation and at the same time I grew up believing in western science.

That belief was shattered when a particular client came forward during the years after having completed a Master degree in Psychotherapy. We share this experience only as a way to say we are all growing, our ideas and beliefs also have great potential to evolve and change.

The client described disturbing feelings of being out of place and struggling with their relationships over many years. As much as they had worked to find a solution, nothing they had ever done by way of learning, travel, education, new friendships, career changes, and seeing many different therapists had helped them resolve this inner feeling of discontent. In truth, as a psychotherapist I was sceptical that my skills were adequate to assist. Relying on basic approaches, we explored a form of mindfulness that included relaxation, meditation and guided visualisation of very simple things like the client's garden or a walk along the beach. Within that fairly contained therapeutic space the person went into a very different place. They talked from a voice quite unlike their own, and described being in what seemed like another country, even another century. In the months that followed we did research that led us to see the client may have had a spontaneous experience of past life regression.

In actual fact, having recorded together the details of several sessions that included an increasing detail of memories, we were able to engage research that led us to conclude the time and place of the memories. It came to light that seemingly spontaneous memories were associated with the historical existence of certain people in another place and time. This did not overly impress me, given that anyone can have exposure to any given information years before, consciously forget the details, and then that information arises in the unconscious mind later in life during a meditation session. Recall of memories appears to be a creative and complex process, and modern brain science is still in its infancy in understanding these phenomena.

But the more significant element, as a psychotherapist, was that the client's lifelong issues were profoundly resolved. It seemed astonishing that long term emotional turmoil and chronic anxiety could be eliminated due to an experience of spontaneous 'past life' memory. This was far outside of any learning gained in the western academe.

Again, whether the experience was about a past life or simply a creative use of the imagination, constructed by the mind and heart to open a pathway to resolution of a deeply disturbing and unresolved issue - who is to say? Because my stance is to respect the beliefs of people we work with, we allowed the client's belief to challenge our perspectives. The work was then about assisting the person in understanding their 'past life memory' as they had experienced this, and then to integrate this knowledge into the present day in such a way that it helped the person to move on with life.

At the end of the day, we did not necessarily believe in reincarnation, the transmigration of soul, or any other belief. Nor did we necessarily believe the client had indeed had a past life regression, or that the issues were resolved from the obvious nature of the revelations and the research process that followed. A rational stance led to consider that it was likely the degree of empathy and openness offered to the client that provided a therapeutic space where the person could feel completely accepted. Instead of denying the client's experience, or suggesting it was irrational or otherwise, and by allowing beliefs to be questioned and to entertain and join within the client's worldview, the client was able to move forward and to feel a small measure of the comfort and fellowship that they had desired during most of their life.

But ultimately, experience led to questioning beliefs. And this was enough to become a bit humbler, and less willing to discount people's experiences and the meaning they draw from them. You might be wise to remember this story as you read through this book, as the basic stance of openness may help you appreciate different cultural and spiritual teachings.

Cultural Respect

For instance, you will find that we use the phrase 'Old Ones of the People' many times. We heard this phrase used by Elders and have read it used in many texts that record some of the Old Stories. The Mi'kmaq are a People who traditionally pay great respect to our Ancestors. We do not walk this life in only a physical world. We walk in a Spiritual Reality that connects us with our Ancestors.

Again, we say this as the belief is based on practical observation of life around us. In all truth, many of us feel, hear and see our Ancestors on a daily basis. They come to us to communicate, to teach, to guide and to protect. Much like the tradition of angels in western Christian traditions, the Ancestors are part of our lives.

We show respect to our Ancestors by leaving them Offerings of Food and Drink in places that we know they come to sit and stay for a while. We do not worship Ancestors, as some have falsely claimed. Our spiritual belief is that there is one Creator, one Great Spirit, one God or Goddess - in traditional ways we do not place a gender on the First Cause.

We feel and relate to the Creator of All through the creation, and in many ways our Ceremony is a deeply spiritual and cultural process that might make others quite uncomfortable. To enter this space, you need to believe in the mystery and wonder of creation. The mindset is open, with feeling, and innocent if not quite childlike. We feel this shows great humility and inner strength to come from the perspective of a child who is open to exploring the nature of the world and to discovery of new meaning. We do this to offer our respect.

We acknowledge Mother Earth as our source of life and that Mother Earth arises from the First Creation by Great Spirit whose Energy can be observed in all things. During Sacred Ceremonies we often offer some of our best food and drink to the Sacred Fire to honour our Ancestors. They bring us closer to Creator through our own bloodline. Because of them we live, have freedom, and enjoy all that life has to offer us. Because of them we also face certain challenges and must deal with unfinished business they have left to our generation.

We see this relationship with our Ancestors, including our Grandparents going back many generations into the deep past, we see this relationship as immediate and part of our lives in very active ways. Not only our human or two legged Ancestors, but we respect familial relationships with many other creatures including four legged, winged, finned, leafy and stone…

M'sit No'koma is a phrase deeply sacred and means 'All My Relations.' All My Relations come to visit us around the hearth-fire of the family lodge. Those who are aware do not need special Ceremony to see, hear and touch these relationships which in the Old Ways were part of everyday life and rarely spoken about – so much so that many of our Nation do not feel that any special spiritual teachings even exist, and these people find it almost insulting and incorrect to focus on spirituality and culture as if the Mi'kmaq People of the past were engrossed within spiritual teachings. Of course, like any culture various people have different experiences and a vast diversity of beliefs, values and attitudes toward life.

Therefore, we offer a corrective comment. By focusing on spirituality and culture over the years we have intentionally done so because of the need for healing of our People and all People of this World. Many will say we do not need healing. And if that is true, I say, wonderful.

For those of us who find comfort in the spirituality and culture of the Old Ones of the People, we do not disrespect anyone by raising this awareness. We do not assume that this is or was the only way to experience life. Far from it. This life-work respects diversity of belief, value and experience above all things.

By looking into the life of the past and bringing forward a feeling of the Sacred, we honour that feeling that exists for many of us within all of life, in every aspect of life, and through all the pathways of life. Respect and honour are central to healing pathways. As such, this work focuses on spirituality and culture as one part of life, not all of life, but certainly as a very important value and belief for many people.

We suggest that to walk slowly in the forest and stop to take a look at a simple leaf is also healing. To look inside the image of the leaf and to allow the heart-mind to experience life unfolding in a sacred manner – this is simple respect and honour. To protect the leaf, tree, and nurture the forest is one of the highest respects and honours that can be shown.

The leaf may remind you of your hand, of the lines of life, and of the stages of birth, growth, maturity and death. In the same way, the leaf can fill you with awe and wonder. This sensation leads you into a sense of worship – within this worship is a feeling of deep humility and wonder that life is so very beautiful and worthy of profound respect. This is not religious not even spiritual. This sense of worship is simple acknowledgement. Life is amazing. Fragile. Interwoven. Beautiful. This is what 'worship' means. We are all so dependent on nature for our life and well-being. In this feeling of worship there is also a sense of thankfulness – to just be in this moment with this leaf – a most simple experience but one that will never happen again in the same way. Ever.

Another person may see and hold the very same leaf but take a different perspective. Those who abide by the material and empirical views of the modern world are themselves limited by western values. If they have taken these values to their logical extreme, they may see only a material object that holds no worth or value to their personal life. They might have a brief moment of sadness when the tree is cut down to make paper for their schoolbook, but they ultimately do not care.

If they are a bit more openminded they may see a biological substance with veins and from their knowledge may dissect the leaf into its properties and elements. If they are a bit more enlightened again, they may see the leaf as part of the living tree. If their views go even further, they may see the leaf as part of a living ecosystem. Although their views would likely be quite limited and hindered by their material assumptions.

For instance, they may overlook how the leaf is related to the birds who come to rest on the tree, and how over decades and even thousands of years the birds have formed a relationship with the species of tree. Or how the leaf and the tree and its neighbours are related to what at first appears to be distant ecosystems, such as the river that flows several miles away, and of how the leaf and the tree are related to the region of shoreline and the more distant ecosystem of the first few miles of ocean.

Essentially, a material and empirical perspective is limited by the underlying assumptions of scope, values and beliefs just as much, if not more, than many other types of beliefs including those that acknowledge the existence of subtle level spiritual and psychic phenomena. This being said, after two decades of intensive study of Indigenous cultural and spiritual beliefs and values around the world we will be so bold as to suggest that culturally grounded spiritual beliefs and traditions tend to hold a well spring of knowledge and wisdom that far surpasses most if not all of the empirical and modern scientific knowledge based in philosophies like materialism and humanism.

Regardless what each person sees, it is difficult to discount either perception. Both hold truth. But not all truth carries the same importance, weight, or implication. Western people always tend to want to be the same as others, and to make others conform to their norms. We western people do not grow up with deep abiding respect for diversity in creation. If we did have these values, most of the damage to the ecosystem we see today would never have been allowed.

Therefore, much of my work in the academe over the past twenty-five years has been to help educate and critique the western perspective, and to bring to bear different cultural and spiritual views that may help to open up new perspectives. How much more exciting and helpful is life when we can allow people different perspectives. But again, I am bold enough to say, how resourceful are your beliefs? If you really test them, do they lead you to a profound happiness and contentment? Or do they lead you to dead ends, more questions, and a sense of dissatisfaction and boredom with life?

In my experience, the western path of knowledge leads to the discontentment of the modern world and is tied up within the consumerism and materialism that makes knowledge just another commodity. Human life and our very being becomes diminished, alienated from what could be a source of great inner peace. In contract, the native path is about experience, quality of life, depth of awareness, and awakening to the wonder of life within and around us. In this context, knowledge has its place. All knowledge needs to be grounded within a local context, as all true knowledge will increase our appreciation of relationships within our own identity, in our intimate relationships, within our families, tribes and nations. False knowledge is always de-contextualised, disconnected, easily used to exploit and abuse, and often deployed to defend and argue the case of rights to use land, water, natural resources and people as a mere expense towards narrowly defined progress.

If I were to go back to the leaf one more time, in the feeling of respect and worship as a form of wonder is also a sense of supplication. In a cultural sense, we know that all creatures are made of the substance of Life. As Life is Sacred, you can see a deep connection between your being and the leaf. We are in fact related, part of one family. The leaf is part of your tribal land, and your people's land comes from Creator. We are charged with the task of being Custodians of the Sacred Land.

By supplication we mean that we can actually communicate with the Leaf as an Entity. As a part of Creation, the Leaf holds an important Spirit, Energy or Essence of the Creator - and even in evolutionary terms the Leaf holds within its structure, substance and form the basic building blocks of all things in nature. The Leaf's very DNA and subatomic structure vibrates with a form of energy and life that even modern science is growing to acknowledge and respect.

Therefore, your belief about your experience of the Leaf leads you to a very rich series of associations, meanings and insights. These provide a wealth of knowledge and wisdom that not only provide satisfaction and connection to your world, but also open up transformative levels of awareness that challenge you to grow and further expand perspectives. But more so, taking a deeper belief gives you a sense of the importance of right actions. We cannot ignore the Leaf because it has become a member of our family. We share a co-responsibility. We are Relations.

Sacred Teachings

The Wigwam of the People

When another force with material or empirical values comes along to not only destroy the Leaf but the Living Tree, and filled with such blindness and greed, may also want to destroy the Living Forest and the Whole Ecosystem of an entire region - you can see why Native people often stand up to fight for the rights of Creation. Our lives hold the treasure of perception and values that have the potential to allow humanity to survive on this planet. But for many people to appreciate this, they first have to examine the limited and hindering nature of their own beliefs and values.

We are one type of consciousness that arises from the Land. All yourself to speak these words that follow and own them as your own:

By sharing a moment with the Leaf as my friend and family member, the Leaf communicates to me that all of life is connected.

In my heart I reach out to the Divine in all of life.

This supplication leads me to the Creator of All beings, by simply witnessing the majesty, beauty and power of this Leafy Brother I am pulled upward into a celestial spiral of light that surrounds and fills my being with the heart-beat of the Mother – the very Energy of Giving Life that makes my body wish to Dance a Most Sacred Dance.

These experiences can remind you of the relationships that the Leaf has with its family, the other leaves, the tree, the roots, other trees, the forest, and the Spirits who dwell in the forest and share in the Sacred Life of this Leaf. Again, read 'sacred' as having infinite value, purpose and destiny.

The very air that enters your lungs could never exist if not for the hard work of Brother Leaf. These realisations fill you with inspiration. If you were to actually be fully and totally aware of the Divine Nature of this one small Leaf, your heart would literally burst open and your mind would completely shut down because our consciousness could never contain the wonder, meaning and truth in this moment. If fully aware, you would fall on my face in complete abandon to your foolishness and lack of ability to grasp the spiritual significance of one seemingly small being in nature. In fact, the majesty, power and influence of this one Leaf suggests your very life depends on the Leafy Nation and all their work to sustain life on this planet.

Even when I consider that the very ground upon which my feet walk must surely be made up of countless generations of leaves who are the Ancestors of this one Leaf who captures my imagination today - I would be so overwhelmed.

I would remember that the earth is made from the Dust of my Ancestors, such that every step is Sacred.

If I were to live in this Awareness my body might go about the world looking completely awake, as I would be in a state of continual bliss and endless reverence.

My every breath would be a Prayer, and every action a form of Ceremony.

These thoughts lead me to understand my own family, and to understand that the Dust of our Ancestors does make up the very soil upon which we live. Oddly enough, these realisations bring me back to the Wigwam because every Wigwam has traditionally been made up of wooden poles taken with respect from this very forest.

For the traditional Mi'kmaq, having the Family Fire within the intimate space of the Wigwam provides an immediate sense of the Ordinary and the Sacredness of All Life. We tend to believe many of our Ancestors lived in a world where it was easier to maintain an attitude of reverence, respect and wonder for all of Life.

Unlike today, it was not fundamentally taboo to have a spirituality. It did not cut to the heart to be so judged by your friends or colleagues for having a different cultural or spiritual belief. Those who study the history tell me there was no separation between the sacred and the profane - all of life was considered Sacred. An attitude of respect and regard for all of Life was part of everyday life. It seems to me our Ancestors minds and hearts were very astute and in-tune with the steady forces of nature.

No person in today's world can live easily in a state of constant reverence and respect. We do not live in a balanced way. And living on the edge of the sacred is extremely challenging. Our path can easily tip to either direction. We have today so many choices. Many subcultures construct strict boundaries and codes of conduct. They attempt to limit risk and liability by setting up controls to guard against the extremes that the modern world affords. The Native Way holds many Teachings. And asks each person to choose their way. There is much freedom. But with great freedom comes even more responsibility.

As you know, for many native people one of the temptations of modern life is alcohol, which is especially difficult and is avoided by anyone seeking a spiritual life. Those who walk a Sacred Path in life will try to avoid many of these experiences by focusing on spiritual teachings and ways of being. Eventually we can focus on the Red Road, the path of spiritual living in the Native Way, and we find we are not avoiding anything at all. We are in fact moving toward that which is good and true. The traditional teachings of the Wigwam provide the Mi'kmaq People with a path toward living a sacred life even while most of us live in modern houses. Instead of going to a church or other place set apart from daily life, the Wigwam suggests that the traditional ways of the People included the sacred within the everyday.

The Fire inside the Wigwam is placed in a shallow pit dug into the Flesh of Mother Earth. The Fire sits in the Centre of the Wigwam. The Centre represents our own Being, when we stand in Sacred Awareness, and when we come into our Power and sense of Purpose in Life. This is an experience of Connecting our Personal Way with our Family, Tribe and with the Nations of Mother Earth. This growth of Awareness and Purpose is the ancient destiny of every Person and given in the Wisdom Teachings of our Elders. The Centre is the Seventh Sacred Direction within the Sacred Circle. The first four represent the Cardinal Directions of East, South, West and North. The fifth and sixth Directions are Above and Below. The Seventh is the Centre.

There is a depth of teachings around these that include many old stories. But for now, we will only suggest that the cosmology of the Mi'kmaq People is traditionally very complex and dynamic. The Sacred Directions are in some ways associated with Many Worlds that exist in parallel dimensions. These together suggest a profoundly interconnected notion of inter-dimensional space. It is unlikely and unclear how much these realisations were a part of everyday culture in the Old Times. But like most indigenous cultures around the world, there are special people of high distinction who practice the Sacred Arts, and whose journey to the Other Dimensions are told in story and legend.

There is certainly discussion of at least six if not eight Sacred Worlds. The map of the universe for the Old Ones of the People included the World Beneath the Earth. The World Beneath the Water. The Water World. The Earth World. The World Above the Earth. The Sky World. The World of Spirits. The World of the Stars. The means to travel these Sacred Worlds relies on learning and practice of the Sacred Arts of Vision Quest. Only the most adept and respected Elders would take their journey to far distant countries to learn the ways of other beings, and to return to the Land of the People, the Red Dirt Country of the Mi'kmaq Nation. In many of those places people were observed as living very different lives, but of facing many of the same challenges we face in our everyday lives. The ability to communicate with other nations includes an ability to speak in the language of the Wolf Nation, the Bear Nation, The Turtle Nation, and/or the Eagle Nation among Many Others.

Certain Wigwams are considered Quite Sacred. These included the Medicine Lodge of the People where sits an Elder whose knowledge and skills are highly valued. Elders hold wisdom in lore, healing, memory of the family history, ability to see into hearts, skills in mediation and counselling, mystical knowledge, and ability to travel to other Worlds and return with wisdom for the People in need. Today Elders keep the Medicine

Lodge alive. Many Elders come together during the summer months to share time and stories. Youth follow them to their meeting places and sit to listen and learn.

The Wigwam itself tells a Sacred Story and is built from thirteen poles. The first four poles used to erect the Wigwam are placed in the Four Cardinal Directions. The first to rise up are the Eastern and Western poles – and only the Eastern pole is dug into a shallow hole within Mother Earth. This hole that is dug is often filled with Sacred Herbs to Honour the Sacred Mother and our Creator. The hole itself is said to be a Sacred Passageway between the Worlds. Upon this pole is rested the doorway of the Wigwam itself. In my writings I often call this doorway a Passageway, because it also represents the simple truth that the physical world around us holds many secrets, and the way we hold our bodies and minds while doing mundane tasks like entering in and out of the Wigwam suggests our core values in life. We may live in modern houses, but we also enter in and out of the Passageway of the House. This threshold means something just as much as the entry of the Old Wigwam. This is why whenever I enter or leave my house, I say a prayer and give thanks for the Sacred Gift of this Place that protects, holds and sustains my life.

The entryway or Passageway into the Wigwam is placed in the Eastern Door. The Place of Honour inside the Wigwam sits in the Western Door, facing the East. To get there, a person must walk around the fire and sit on the other side facing the entry. When the Wigwam is being built, around the four poles are placed all the others. These poles also represent the Moons of the Year. Others have said the number also represent nine poles for the months of birthing to honour the Women of the Nation, plus the four cardinal directions which suggest a foundational Male Energy meant to serve and protect the Women who are the Heart of the Family, and thus the Heart of the Mi'kmaq Nation. Because the Men traditionally may have raised the Four Pillars it is said that the Women complete the Circle, and fill out the Circle with their love, wisdom and spiritual Medicine.

In the Old Ways of the People, some say that Women were the leaders of the Mi'kmaq Nation. Others say that both men and women held roles of leadership and anyone of merit could become an elected Chief. All who were worthy including children could become respected for their unique insight and gifts and may be considered an Elder among the People. In this way, the Elder is respected not for age but for the quality of their being. Likewise, the Spirit Elder of the Wigwam is suggested to be the Ancient Grandmother Turtle. She guards the Northern Door. She too has thirteen sections on her back that are said to represent the thirteen tribes of humanity. These were seeded from the Original Teachings given to the Mi'kmaq People in the Time before Time.

In another story, the first Pole set in the Eastern Door represents the child and youth on their journey to find the self and their sacred purpose in life. They will journey around the cycle of the moons many times before coming back to their Inner Truth and coming to terms with their Life Quest or the Meaning of their Work in this World. Usually this journey takes them to their thirteenth year of life when they are ready to undertake a Sacred Initiation into Adulthood. In these teachings, the Wigwam itself suggests a developmental path through life that provides the wisdom needed to meet the challenges of human growth and change.

Additionally, the number of poles in the Wigwam represents the Wisdom Teachings and these suggest the core qualities and values that make up a good life. Among these are practicing humility, listening, respect, patience, forgiveness, learning, sharing, honour, truth, humour, openness, creativity, and kindness.

The Wigwam itself came to represent a Spirit Being because of the Energy of Life associated with this Place. Through the top of the wigwam the Life Energy of the Sky can be felt and channels through to the Earth. The Eastern Door is grounded in the Earth and so forms a complete circuit of Energy. The Fire within represents the Life Breath in our Bodies. The Smoke is Sacred ~ Given to Creator and Honouring our Ancestors who dwell in the World of the Stars and The World Beyond. In these ways, the Wigwam is the perfect everyday place and Sacred Space. The Seeker can either stay in the mundane everyday world or can engage with Sacred Journey to the height of their ability and skill. Likewise, the Wigwam can be associated with the energy centres of the human body. I have for many years now considered the connections between various healing models around the world, and the depth of wisdom available regarding traditional Mi'kmaw cosmology and natural healing methods. These require a separate discussion and are worth exploring. Suffice it to say that working with wholistic healing and embodied energetic forms of healing are a profoundly important part of traditional Medicine knowledge, not yet lost because Creator gives to each generation Elders borne to us who remember aspects of these Old Ways that still exist within the bloodlines and wisdom of the People. We can cleanse and open these streams within our psyche and within the human energy system that parallel the streams, rivers and bodies of water in nature.

My life is only a pale reflection of the depth of knowledge, experience and wisdom of our native Elders, Medicine Keepers, Medicine Men and Woman, Keepers of Story, Keepers of the Fire, and Keepers of the Sweat Lodge and other Ceremony. I am not an Elder and have never claimed to be one. My work for the Nation is as a student, scribe and servant who with a sense of duty provides my writings for the wellbeing of others. And while the Circle of Elders meeting in Sacred Council bestowed upon me the responsibility of carrying Sacred Medicine and associated Teachings, my work during this skin-time reflects the memories and insights given to me by my native namesake and those Elders with whom I have been honoured to share time. Nothing I have written is without consultation with the Guides given to me for this purpose. In this way I must say that my work has been for the Seventh Generation, those who I will never meet face to face, which very likely includes you the reader. In this way, my work is produced for the youth of our Nation and other nations who may one day decide to seek the Medicine Path for insight and guidance.

    My reconnection to the Mi'kmaw Way has deeply enriched my life, given peace and purpose, and opened pathways I never knew existed before. These Teachings have reconciled the conflicts of the modern age within me and allowed my body-mind-heart and my spirit a steady and sure direction. Engaging in Sacred Ceremony has taught me to know myself, to hear my inner voice, to become empowered, to heal the hurts of the past, and to move a bit more slowly and gracefully through the world. In all of these ways, my writing is given back first to my People as a resource and in humility. I know without any doubt that my words are inadequate to express, describe or manifest a vision of the Power and Truth found in the Mi'kmaw Traditions of the Eastern Door. In truth, there are no words in the English language to express this connection.

    Symbolically speaking, like most of my kin I have lived most of my mundane life in a modern house. But also, like many of my kin, I have kept a Wigwam close by, to enter into a different way of being. At times this space provides a place to rest, to talk, to share, and to eat delicious meals. At other times, the Wigwam becomes a Medicine Lodge. And in those hours of Vision, the Sacred Arts of spiritual journey can be explored fully. Over time my house itself has become the Wigwam, and this too is symbolic of taking on a more sacred approach to life over the years.

As my hair grows grey and falls out, my body changes and grows a bit more tired, and I sense the days remaining on this planet might be less than given to me in past, a greater inner freedom emerges to speak my truth and vision without fear of what others will think. Sensing these changes my choices over the past several years led me into greater travel, personal change and solitude. In seeking the lonely ways my purpose was to find the voice that helped me to complete this work. In many respects this was done for the youth of tomorrow, for my nieces and nephews, for my grandnieces and grandnephews. This work is for the members of my family in Eskasoni First Nation, Waycobah First Nation, and Bear River First Nation and especially for our youth who may benefit from reading these reflections. This work is for people who at some stage during their life decide to seek out the Medicine Ways of the People. By offering these Teachings first to the Mi'kmaq Nation during 2007-2009, the writings had time to be tested and questioned into existence. Now they will have more time to be reflected upon and preserved for the future.

How to enjoy this collection

This collection is based on a three-year cycle. You may choose to read one entry each month. If you do, each entry is most useful to read during the New or Dark Moon. If you do this, the New Moon can become a time of reflection and growth. As you reach the Full Moon, you can celebrate your experience in some way that is unique to you. In this approach, you can pace yourself through the three-year cycle.

Or you can easily continue reading right through, as I myself would very likely do during a first run. And later on, you might decide to pace yourself through the cycle while following the suggestions below on working with your personal spiritual quest. This process can have lasting benefits in your life including growth in awareness. By allowing the traditional teachings to seep into your consciousness and feed your soul and spirit, the more you put in, the more you will get from the experience.

Because the first version of these stories was published in a regional monthly paper, the Mi'kmaw moon cycle used fits in with the twelve months of the year. I decided to leave it this way because the twelve months of the year provide the easiest means to pace someone through a learning cycle that corresponds with the calendar we use in the modern world. It is not important that you stay on track with these exercises. If you miss a month or more, that is OK. If you put down the process and leave it for a few years, that is also good. The key is to listen to your heart and attend to your own life-unfolding.

The spirit and heart-felt feeling of the collection begins and ends with the invitation to enter the Sacred Medicine Lodge. In the Wigwam of the People, you are invited to listen to the Teachings offered while listening to your Thoughts and Feelings. Become aware that your inner voice is also Sacred. Given to you for a purpose. The process is about respect for yourself. If anything does not ring true, say thank you very much, and put that thing aside. Use what is helpful to you.

To assist your internal learning process, I encourage you to write in a journal and record your thoughts, feelings, insights and questions as you go along. I have personally kept a journal since 1978. The process of journal writing assisted me in many ways to learn about myself, my feelings, and to reflect on life and meaning. The process of writing personal reflections led me to observe people around me and learn how people operate, what they struggle with, and how they grow, change and heal from past hurts. Like anyone entering on a journey of discovery, the insights led to certain pathways that were of most interest and over time these interests led toward a sense of identity, destiny and purpose in life. Journal writing opened to me my life-path because I was willing to listen and was committed to this journey. At each turn, I was willing to say yes to the task at hand. Sometimes this task was very simple - like washing the dishes for my parents who worked all day to provide food and shelter. Other times the task was to take on debt to get an education. Later in life, to pay off that debt and move on with new tasks.

At times Life asked me to leave behind many things to walk toward the Light ahead of me. To feel and see these challenges clearly took me into the woods of Mi'kma'ki to sit by the lake and streams. At each major turn of my life the courage to say yes came from times of solitude and prayer in the wooded environments of my Ancestors and my present-day family. Seeking the quiet solitude of the woods was not easy. As anyone will say who has tried to clear your mind and to truly listen to the hidden voice of Creator, moving from the busy everyday life into the quiet stillness of the forest takes time and patience. Then the role of journal writing helped me to record and understand the images, impressions and voices given to me during those quiet hours...

You may think journal writing is not native or indigenous. You might base this assumption on the idea that books, pens and paper are things from the modern world. But in a sense, while you are right here, you are also wrong. My Ancestors wrote with different tools. They wrote on birch bark and carved in stone and drew pictographs in stone. They told stories, shared teachings, gave warnings, sent messages and letters, and they also recorded events in history through the clever use of beaded belts called Wampum. The Mi'kmaq Nation was so adept at writing and recording ideas, that they developed their own unique written language that uses pictographs on par with the ancient language of Egypt. Few people today know how to use this written language. But Elders still live who have used this form of writing. Many people are working hard to keep the Mi'kmaw spoken language alive. Your modern life today may be much more connected with your Ancestors than you might at first assume – so think again. We are all connected. Time and space do not separate us, but rather they bind us closer together.

You may want to look up the dates for new moons and full moons as these are the focus of the reflections in this series. For your personal use you may also copy the Moon Cycle Calendar found at the back of this book and post the resource on your wall or in your Sacred Space. We provide the calendar for the next six-year cycle. After that you will need to do your own research to find the timing of the New and Full Moons.

The second quarter moon, which occurs during the waning or diminishing moon cycle (after the full moon), is a time of rest and letting go. For this reason, there are no reflections during this phase. Every garden needs a fallow time to recover, to allow the nutrients to grow in the soil, and to rest before the next growing season. This is also true of the Sacred Moon cycles, and of the human being, as our Spirits walk through similar Circles of Being that follow the Moon Cycles.

In traditional culture, spirituality is woven into the fabric of daily life such that it is sometimes difficult to identify exactly what this means. Sharing spiritual teachings is felt to be part of the normal process of life and learning and may not be identified as special or unique. In modern native cultures like many others around the world, spiritual teachings have become somewhat separate and distinct from everyday life. For this reason, it is even more important to keep a balance and to offer times of celebrating and honouring spiritual insights.

When you get to the First Quarter, when the Moon is half grown, consider what ways you can grow yourself by taking on the teachings offered. Write in your journal about your experiences and record your journey each day. When the Moon is Full, take time to celebrate and engage Sacred Ceremony as you see fit. There will be suggestions throughout the readings which you can take on, try and play with, or ignore as you choose. Spiritual work is a very personal affair, and no one has any right to tell you what to do. There are few very strict rules, as we are all Children of Creator, given a deep spiritual dignity, freedom and responsibility to act within ethics of care, love, consideration and compassion toward all beings. If your actions parallel these ethical values, nothing you do can be absolutely wrong.

At the time of the Full Moon, you can remember the spiritual teachings for this moon cycle, write about them in your own words, reflect how they are a part of your life and experience already. See what insights come up. And afterwards, you can re-read the teachings for this Moon recorded in this book. How much did you take on without even realising it? Most things native rely on communicating between the head and the heart – living in a balanced way. We walk in balance and beauty. Take the teachings into your heart and mind. Take them out into the open air. Take them to work and play. See what emerges in your lifeworld. Be curious and childlike and look for lessons hidden behind different experiences. Observe your world in its physical and concrete forms and read life around you like a book with many lessons, as mundane or as profound as you wish to go in your feelings and thoughts. This is very much an Ancient Science ~ an Indigenous Methodology.

The key parts are observing with open senses, eyes, ears and heart. Listening with two ears – one hearing what is obvious and one hearing what is hidden or suggested. Pondering and digesting involves allowing the lifeworld to be both practical and metaphorical. The metaphor is something that is obvious but suggests something very different. For example, an apple may be a food to ingest and enjoy. But the metaphor of apple to someone may mean a gift from a friend, an invitation to celebrate life, a temptation that leads to a downfall, or a new adventure waiting to be explored.

So, any one thing in life can mean a whole range of ideas and meanings depending on each person's intuition and sense of 'this is right for me now.' When that feeling comes up, you can accept it and learn from it. It may be helpful to literally ask the Moon Mother 'what wisdom do you have for me now in my life?' And listen for what arises in your heart. Often our inner self wishes to help us and is only waiting for us to ask the right question. Then an idea, thought, feeling, word, sound or image might come up within awareness. At first you may not understand the meaning with your conscious mind, that part of your brain focused on immediate logical or practical awareness. But give it time. It may take a while, even weeks. But eventually the meaning will come clear. From the depth of the subconscious self, arises help for those who listen, feel and look.

Sometimes, I have experienced messages coming up within my dreams and visions that did not make sense to me at the time they came to me. This is another reason why a journal helps. I wrote them down. In some cases, several years passed before the meaning became clear. Then I remembered the vision, image or teaching that had been given to me. And because of the writing, going back and looking for the context of when that came to me provided insights that may have been lost otherwise. In older times similar processes were engaged including collecting special objects, like a Sacred Stone, or Feather, or Animal Hide, which embodied the time, context and memories of a Special Teaching. These reminded the individual of something important. The journal to me is a very Sacred Space, because it can contain the most important insights that come from Spirit and bring us closer to Creator as well as to our Divine Purpose in life.

We are funny people today. We have lost our way. We might think, for example, that a book made of white bleached paper is nothing special at all. We may look at it and not feel any sacred feelings. We have come to look at life and the objects around us as completely lifeless, devoid of meaning. We have lost a sense of the Spirit of Life in all things within and around us. This is tragic and a great loss. This leaves us without imagination, and without allies and helpers. This leaves us feeling alone and without direction, purpose and meaning. Human beings are meant to live in community, in family. We are relational beings.

This is why, for me at least, having a Sacred Journal has become an important symbolic and spiritual discipline that helps me ask different questions each day – what did I learn today that was important? What did I see, feel or touch that was Sacred and Meaningful? How can I grow and become a better person through my experience today? What is Creator speaking to me through the events of the day or night? What most simple thing might become a point of meaning and strength for me today?

This discipline can be very difficult for some people at first. Spiritual teachings often tell people to take baby steps. For instance, when you meditate and quiet your mind, begin with only five minutes and have a good experience rather than trying to make it half an hour and going nuts because your mind is racing or distracted, and you then feel bad about your effort. This is a helpful teaching. You need to take what is good for you right now and let go of the rest. The important part is really your heart-intention.

But I find that most people actually just dive right in and try to do the whole nine yards all at once. This is human nature. We instinctively feel what we need, and we know what is good for us, and we want it all right now, because life is short, and discipline is not easy to maintain in the long run. We tend to let go of things and move on. This is built into our subconscious awareness; we just know this about ourselves. So, I tend to think, grasp onto the moment and live it to the fullest. Why not? If your goal is to meditate, do it for half an hour at least or take a full hour! Make it very special. Use music, or candles, or incense, or burn Sacred Native Herbs like Sweet Grass or Sage. Give a Tobacco Offering to Mother Earth before and after the Meditation. Simply take a pinch of Sacred Tobacco and lay it beside a tree or on the earth in a spot people will not be walking. Go with the flow of your Meditation, and really enjoy it to the full.

In the same way, if you decide to write in a journal make it very special for yourself. Search out journals with lovely covers and nice pages, maybe something with more natural paper. Sometimes I would write special messages on a piece of Birch Bark that I collected from a large tree, dried and made into a form of paper. This technique was familiar to my Ancestors. They wrote messages on Birch Bark to send to family and tribal relations who were far away, usually carried by a traveller or messenger on foot. Expanding the idea of a place to record and remember special teachings makes a journal very flexible. For Native people, collecting a Medicine Bundle is like a Sacred Journal.

A Medicine Bundle is a collection of Sacred Objects that contain many teachings, meanings and memories. Each item comes to you at a particular time in life. In my Bundle, each item is wrapped in special cloth. Even the cloth holds special memories and came to me during particular times of life. An Elder once gave me a cloth she had made with special Red on one side and a Seashell pattern on the other side. She offered this handmade gift to me for the Sacred Pipe, and so I use this cloth as a base upon which to lay the other items during Sacred Ceremony. Only recently it dawned on me that she gave me this cloth with Seashells because she saw that one day I would be living inland and far away from the Ocean. For the Mi'kmaq the Ocean is an ever-present Helper, Friend, Guide and Challenger. We grow up by the Sea, and this is in our blood. Her cloth gives me comfort and holds the energy of the Mi'kmaw Waters of North Eastern Turtle Island.

When I realised that I needed cloths to protect and hold the Sacred Energy of various objects, I began to collect Red Cloths. Red is a very sacred colour to many Indigenous Peoples, and a Sacred Ceremonial Colour to the Mi'kmaq. I also collected special tea towels with very lovely designs of birds and animal life, and special silk cloths. Silk is a unique fabric that is very soft, pure and strong in weave so keeps out negative energies and protects the objects inside.

Every person's Medicine Bundle is extremely unique, but many do contain similar objects as above and may include items like Sacred Pipes, Sacred Native Flutes, Animal Hides and other Sacred Animal items like Teeth, Bone or Feathers. These are treated with utmost respect and form part of Sacred Ceremonial Prayer or Meditation. Often the physical object becomes like a channel or Sacred Presence through which an Energy, Teaching or Impression is shared with the person in Ceremony. After time the Sacred Object becomes part of one's family, part of the fabric of one's Ceremonial daily life.

We say we need to 'Sit with the Medicines' from time to time, to bring our lives back into spiritual balance and harmony.

By Sitting with the Medicines, we become whole again, we heal, and we gain strength by being together with our Spiritual Family whose Presence we experience within and through the Sacred Objects given to us during various times of our lives to help us.

Be aware of the energies of the Earth around you. Come closer to the Earth whenever possible. Sit on and feel the dirt between your fingers and toes. If it is cold and there is snow, enjoy the cold. Allow yourself to struggle with the cold and learn how to have a relationship with the cold. Write in your journal how you are growing in awareness through the Relationships with Life around you and inside of you.

Conclusion

These writings are offered as wisdom teachings to assist you and other people in today's world. They were first written for the People of the Eastern Door of Turtle Island, the Mi'kmaq Nation. After revision and updating they are offered to anyone interested and seeking a life that is more balanced and more at-peace.

This book is written from a personal voice in a reflective and spiritual tone. The readings are meant to speak to the heart and imagination of the reader. The book is meant to be a personal development companion to help the reader learn and grow. The original intention of the Eagle Medicine Column was to speak to my People from this place of Ceremonial and Cultural Respect. Experiences, observations and opinions are shared during this narrative. Opinions and views shared here are entirely my own and do not speak for any particular elders, communities, organisations or bodies.

Although many statements in this book suggest knowledge of the Mi'kmaq People, even here my intention is not to speak for our People. My only intention is to speak from my heart and mind as one. Please allow my words to reflect my personal perspectives only. But more so, please be aware that my primary purpose is to offer you these writings to awaken in you many perspectives, questions, insights and a deeper personal awareness.

With respect for different opinions, allow me to clarify several questions. There are many perspectives on Mi'kmaw culture. The views in this book come from personal experience and are highly influenced by my identity as a Mi'kmaw person. My approach focuses on contemporary life and culture. I am not an historian. While many comments reflect on the cultural identity of people today while reflecting on their heritage, there are no statements in this book that can be taken as 'historical truth' in the classic sense of the phrase.

In my knowledge of historiography, there are many debates on the validity of all historical and ethnographic writings. Given the controversial nature of colonisation, and of the often-one-sided misuse of Mi'kmaw cultural knowledge within European science and scholarship, naturally people today are weary and demand to know where a writer is coming from.

In some respects, my approach might be seen by some readers as reflecting on history and culture. However, my focus on culture does not include an interest in history in any classic sense. The only historical value of this book might arise in future generations when people are wondering what did we tend to believe today, during this generation?

This book is not an academic work and does not cite historical references outside of the oral tradition that come to my awareness. Knowledge of the oral tradition comes from my family and personal experience. This work does not reflect a research agenda. Regardless, in exceeding the expectations of the Mi'kmaq Ethics Watch I have donated this work to the Mi'kmaq Resource Centre, Cape Breton University, under the guidance of Elected Chiefs and Respected Elders. This commitment on my part is to give back to the community the knowledge gained from personal *and* professional work.

As to history, my basic stance is that we can never know for certain what our Ancestors did or believed during the past. The best we can do is reconstruct our identity today based on a unique contemporary view of our history and culture. This everyone can engage, own and create.

Another important point. The Mi'kmaq have survived over five hundred years of often hostile interactions with other cultures. Looking back in my family history we were literally torn apart by political upheaval. Especially during the Acadian expulsion many Mi'kmaq family members were sent away to other parts of the continent. In those days we were one family. We were united by the Sacred Bonds of Marriage. Only a small remnant remained. One of my Grandfathers refused to leave, one Charles Richard. I am told that during the expulsion he retreated to the woods of New Brunswick with our Mi'kmaq cousins. After conflicts had ceased, he moved to a remote area on the Eastern Shore and founded Charlos Cove. From his line my grandmother and father were born. Later, the Indian Act further separated kin from kin.

After eons of hardship my generation seeks reconnection and solidarity. We are literally fourteen generations from 1652, when Michel Richard settled and married a Mi'kmaw bride. He lived in Belle Isle near Port Royal, close to Bear River First Nation. My family includes the following family names known in the historical record to represent Mi'kmaq people who became also French Acadian through marriage: Muis/Meuse, Bourg, Doucet/Doucette, Bonnevie, Lord, Wolf/Wulf, Therese, Petitpas, Hebert, Doiron, Decoste, Pelrine, and L'Avantier. I am proud of my heritage and am proud within my Mi'kmaq family. My life-work honours all of our Ancestors from whatever country they come.

Regarding the use of 'Mi'kmaq' and 'Mi'kmaw', the former is a plural noun and used when speaking of more than one person or a whole people, hence the Mi'kmaq Nation. Mi'kmaw is a singular noun, such as, 'I am Mi'kmaw.' Mi'kmaw also serves as an adjective describing a noun, such as, 'I am a Mi'kmaw person.' This convention follows the Francis Smith Orthography completed during the 1980s. As my connections extend into Quebec, other Mi'kmaw words may not follow this orthography.

In summary, allow me to say that from personal development arises forms of spiritual awakening. This is really seeing clearly, in whatever way you see and put words to your life. We come alive through this process. We begin to live in purpose and destiny. Living your dream in life is no small project. This is a spiritual awareness. In the Spirit of the Sacred Sunrise Ceremony, I wish you well on your journey. May this new day bring you every blessing and peace.

Sacred Teachings

The First Moon Cycle: Year One

Joseph Randolph Bowers

Kesik/Winter Moons

January Punamujuiku's Frost Fish Moon

Pjila'si ~ Welcome, come in, sit down.

Welcome to the Medicine Lodge. In this place you will be invited to sit upon Mother Earth. Naturally, when I keep the Lodge in a Wigwam, we do indeed sit upon Mother Earth. But when the Lodge is kept open in a home, or any other place, naturally we might sit in comfy chairs. Regardless where the

Lodge is set up, certain protocols make the Space Sacred, direct the Power and keep people Safe.

Part of the traditional protocol suggests that the Space of Ceremony includes many types of activities outside of what people might think of as formal ceremony. For example, traditional Ceremonial practice will include the discourse of discussion, listening, hearing, perceiving, seeking and vision-questing while also activities like Gathering, Preparation of the Medicines, Opening the Directions, Honouring the Ancestors, Smoking of the Pipe, Sharing the Pipe, Tending the Fire, and Burning of Sacred Herbs, to name a few.

The context in the traditional way indicates that the Medicine Keeper lives a Sacred Life of Honour, so that the Sacred Place of the Medicine Lodge in particular is a Consecrated Space, set aside for Spiritual Practice. Normally in this Way of Peace the Medicine Lodge would be free from any spirits of harm and compromise. This would include being free of the spirits of alcohol, abuse and trauma. A sense of the purification and existing purity of the Space would exist for those who visit – suggesting that the Medicine Person lives a life of high degrees of dedication, self-development, and gradual change that builds up over time the Pure Energies of Love and Spiritual Power from whom all good and balanced healing, insight and vision arise.

These thoughts and feelings we share now are dedicated to the Frost Fish Moon which is celebrated by the traditional Mi'kmaq People of the Eastern Door of Turtle Island, or North America. Frost Fish Moon celebrates and provides warning. This time of year, we celebrate the Powers of the Northern Door where the depth of winter and darkness are a time to bring families together – both for survival of the harsh conditions and to build intimate family relations around the Central Fire – the hearth and the heart of family. In the Old Ways of the People, we live in the Wigwam with the Central Fire a daily and nightly companion. Around the Fire our family gathers, stays warm, prepares food, eats, and shares stories, sleeps and wakes up to the next day. The Wigwam is surpassed only with the spirit of the Long House when families gather together in a larger structure to share their lives and the natural resources of Mother Earth.

The Frost Fish Moon holds a warning as well. When the time of darkness is upon us, we must be well prepared to survive. We need to have set provisions for the Long Winter and the Short Day, because by our stores we will have enough resources and Medicines to endure. This is traditionally a time when Mother Nature weans us of dependence. The darkness symbolises the letting go of the Body to attain the Spirit. It is not surprising that many of our Elders have traditionally sought the Spirit World during the Long Darkness of the North, when the Deep Frost takes a permanent hold upon the Land and often does not let go until the Spring.

We are the People of the Dawn, the Wabanaki. Our Spiritual purpose is to Guard the Entry to the Sacred Circle, which sits in the East. In this way, we have Tended the Garden of Turtle Island by being Her Messenger of the Dawn and by Greeting the Dawn in Ceremony since the Beginning of Time on behalf of all the People of Turtle Island.

Each Cardinal Direction, East, South, West and North, are called Doorways because they represent passages into other Worlds or Realms of Power. Through Ceremonial Practice we can enter these Doors and pass into new experiences of living life within the Ceremonial Vision. We use our imagination and allow ourselves to travel while still being grounded in our bodies in the here and now. We do this in part by setting the boundaries of safety that govern our Sacred Circle. The Circle is a Place of Comfort and Safety. We naturally bring whatever Energies are within us when we Open the Circle and Set the Sacred Directions in Motion. For this reason, we need to purify our bodies, minds, hearts and spirits by burning Sacred Herbs. Many say that no bad energies can enter the Circle without first being invited. I rather like to think Creator gives all good things for our purpose, and we learn from everything.

Sacred Sage is used to Cleanse of all confused Energies. Sage allows those Spirits and Energies to pass away from our bodies and go back to Mother Earth to be used in Good Ways in the Creation of Life. Sacred Cedar is used to Purify our bodies and the Sacred Space we will make for Ceremony. Sacred Sweet Grass is used to Honour the Ancestors and brings a wonderfully Sweet feeling of contentment and healing. Sacred Tobacco is used to offer heartfelt prayers to Creator and to bless Mother Earth and is used as a sacrificial offering as Tobacco is very Sacred, Potent and Powerful. Many teachings exist for each of the Sacred Herbs, and like everything in Native culture, you can take the surface and simple ways at face value, or you can choose to keep seeking the deeper truths and mysteries that tend to be less obvious and less known, but are nonetheless part of the Wisdom Traditions of the People.

Living in this Sacred Way holds many demands. It is not an easy path for some people. Native people are no different. We struggle with temptations and ways of life that are not conducive to the deeper mysteries of Sacred Ceremonial Life. For example, over time this path has asked me to change my lifestyle. When I first took on the Sacred Gifts of my Elders, including a Sacred Medicine Pipe and a Sacred Eagle Feather, I was very excited and learned so much within the first year of Carrying this Sacred Medicine. During that year I slept with the Pipe nearby, held safe in the Medicine Bundle. The Pipe would speak to me in my dreams and gave me many teachings during that first year. This often disrupted my sleep. This changed my lifestyle very much and was challenging.

As I began to understand the Power of the Medicines and of Ceremonial Life, the teachings of abstaining from alcohol grew in my awareness. At first, Elders told me of the need to not drink. I took this on face value and respected the teaching. Intellectually I understood the history of substance abuse, and the rationale that at least four days must be given without drinking before and after any Sacred Ceremony. This held many lessons for me. But over time, as I experienced more and learned more, the teaching began to live inside of me. At first, when I drank and respected the four days before and after Ceremony, I found that I was a bit more aware of how the body needed to recover from drinking even a small quantity of alcohol. When I did take alcohol and was later called into Ceremony by an Elder before the four days was up the outcome was extremely uncomfortable. This happened once when I was asked to take part in Sweat Lodge Ceremony.

At the time, the Elder was very astute. Indeed, I had drank a low-alcohol beer two nights before. I had forgotten, because I was not very aware during that time due to many stresses and my lack of spiritual discipline. The Elder pulled me up when I sat on the ground of the Lodge. She pointed her rattle and commented that I had been drinking or taking drugs. I had to think for a moment. Then looked down and realised my mistake. I said yes, I had a 'low-alcohol beer the other night, I think it was two nights ago.' She suggested she could smell the alcohol on me. She paused. I said, 'I am so sorry. I mean no disrespect. I will leave and learn from my mistake.' Then she let me know that I was welcome to stay in the Sweat Ceremony but was not allowed to touch any Sacred Objects. My actions would mean that the full benefits of the Ceremony would be lost to me, and that suffering would follow my actions. But this was my

Medicine Path, and I was meant to learn from my mistakes. When being asked if I would stay, I replied, 'Wela'lia (thank you), I will stay and learn.'

The lessons learned were many. For one, I learned more humility. It was humbling to be called up by a highly respected Elder, in front of other Elders who I loved and admired. Among them were Elders who were present the day that I was entrusted with the Sacred Pipe, a couple years before. While I know they did not judge me, I could feel their disappointment. During the prayers, I felt their strength, resilience, and their assistance by just allowing me to stay with them. This taught me a lesson of patience, loving kindness, firmness of purpose, discipline and commitment. From that day forward my thinking changed. I came to respect even more the seriousness of my commitment to spiritual life.

Physically life changed as well. Over the time since walking with the Sacred Medicines, when I drank alcohol it threw my spirit out of balance. This was probably always the case, but I did not have a way to understand. Alcohol changes the physical body. We are more prone to getting colds, flues and to suffer from fatigue. Early on, we might drink more before we feel these things. But during our spiritual walk, and as we get older, we become more sensitive. More aware. Physical disruptions in our body are more quickly registered in our Spirit. We become more sensitive to the Spiritual Power of Alcohol and its physical, emotional and social demands.

Alcohol carries the Spirit of Equal Measure. This Entity demands payment where payment is due. The same can be said for Tobacco. When the substance is disrespected, the Dark Spirit manifests in personal, familial and tribal hardship. The Native Way reserves the use of Medicines to the most Sacred of Ceremony. This is why Alcohol and Tobacco are misunderstood. As Medicines, they are not meant to be abused.

Alcohol is used as a Medicine in the Christian Mass for those of our Nation who honour the Christian traditions. And for others, Raising the Cup of Blessing in the Sacred Ceremony of the Old Tribal Ways of the Celtic Nations may also be an experience that a few of our People enjoy.

In my path, the more I learned about the Energy and Power of Alcohol, the more I felt to not drink. This choice is in Solidarity with my Elders and our Medicine Tradition. After a time, I also decided to not have alcohol in my home, because my home became a Medicine Lodge. If friends bring alcohol, I respectfully ask them to keep it in their car or to put the bottle by the fence. There is now no dividing line between doing a secular activity like drinking and a Sacred activity like Ceremony. All of Life is Sacred. And Life demands respect.

Many people do not take up the Spiritual Path because they fear giving up things, they feel they enjoy now. My response is well, everyone makes their own decision. But for me, there is no absolute. I can decide today to enjoy a party that a friend might decide to have, and at the party I might decide to drink. Afterward I might suffer from the effects of that choice, and hopefully I might learn from that experience. This is the process of life unfolding. Live and learn. If you truly love within each choice in life, there is ultimately little harm done. But over time, I have learned that when I drink any quantity of alcohol, I tend to feel slightly different. The mind feels clouded. This feeling makes me uncomfortable. Life is a Sacred Journey. So, we need clarity of mind. There is no secular time or down time anymore. Every moment I am praying in one way or other, simply by enjoying a sunrise or sunset, or enjoying a delicious meal with my partner. Life for me needs as much clarity in perception as possible, and this gives more peace of mind.

Others have told me that I have been chosen by the Sacred Medicines of the Mi'kmaq Nation. Because of this, the

Medicines do not abide with the fire water of the European Nations. A Celtic Elder and Monk once told me that fire water is Sacred Medicine to the Celt when used in Ceremony. My response was that drinking is normally not a Ceremony, nor is it Sacred. He responded that from the Old Celtic perspective Alcohol is a Medicine, and like any Medicine it must be taken with great care and can be easily abused. He reminded me of Tobacco and how this too is a Sacred Medicine to native people and can also be easily abused as an addictive substance when the First Intention of the Creator for the People was to use the Herb as a Sacred Doorway to the Spiritual Realms.

He reminded me that when we Offer Tobacco to Mother Earth, we are opening a spiritual Doorway that allows into our lives a Sacred Awareness and a Gift. We are interconnected. Our prayer and our life-force are interdependent with every other living and non-living thing. The Gift is that we might think we have something to Offer but in reality, we have Nothing. We are as naked as we were when we first came out of our Mother's Womb. We are indeed given whatever we have by Creator and asked to give that back freely – to remain empty, naked and open-handed. We give the Tobacco to acknowledge our complete dependence on all of Life around us, on Creator, for everything we have, know, do and wish to experience in future.

Then the Celtic Monk reminded me that Consecrated Wine is used during the Ceremony of the Mass at the most Sacred Moment, echoing back to Ancient Aboriginal Ceremonies of the Celtic Nations where the Cup of the Goddess was held in equally high esteem and shared among friends and family as a Cup of Blessing filled with the fruits of the earth. In this way, the Alcohol is made Sacred and does not harm. He said this is perhaps similar to the way that Tobacco is smoked in the Sacred Pipe of the Mi'kmaq People but does not harm, because this has become a Smoke of Blessing. All things used in balance and for spiritual purposes bring about peace, health and contentment.

For Native people, when a Medicine Man blesses Sacred Herbs and when using Sacred Smoke for healing and other types of Ceremony, these Herbs take on a different meaning. They embody an intensity of Spirit and Presence from the Creator. They are Sacred. For this reason, to the surprise of many, sometimes people who have trouble with allergies and other illnesses are able to abide with Sacred Medicines without any trouble. Naturally, great care must be taken and sensitivity to individual's needs attended to. In each case, the Medicine Woman will change her approach to match the energy and life force of the seeker.

Reflection

During this New Moon consider for yourself what Sacred Ceremony might mean to you? While you may not have a way to conduct such a Ceremony now, consider what you might like to learn or experience in future. Give this intention to Creator in some way. Write your feelings and thoughts in your journal. Allow the waxing/growing moon to take your prayers and intentions to Creator and transform them into something tangible in your life.

When the moon reaches the First Quarter during the waxing cycle, take a moment to do something meaningful for you. Offer Tobacco to give thanks for the growing changes in your life, even if these changes are hidden from obvious view they are still happening around and within you. Or offer a Flower, or a bit of Pine needles or a pinch of Cedar. Do something to mark the transition as a sign of the growth of new things in your life. Then write in your journal.

When it comes to the Full Moon, take these thoughts and review them, maybe read this entry again and see how it sits with you. What lessons do you wish to bring forward in your life? Acknowledge how the Moon in fullness represents your own projects, plans, hopes and visions coming to their own degree of fulfilment over time. Celebrate life in all its fullness by having a delicious meal, or a bubble bath with nice music, or an intimate sensual encounter with your partner, or some other way of Celebrating. Over time you will learn that Celebrating from the Heart is one of the Most Sacred events of life. When you learn to Celebrate well it means your inner person is strong, you are balanced and at peace, and you can fully enjoy all that life has for you. M'sit No'koma, Ta'ho (All My Relations, So Be It/It is Done).

Joseph Randolph Bowers

February Apiknajit Snow Blinder Moon

Pjila'si ~ Welcome, come in, sit down.

In this Medicine Lodge today we will honour first the gift of Sage and purify our bodies, minds, hearts and spirits. Take the Sage and allow the smoke to flow over you. While holding the large Seashell that holds the burning Sage, move your hand through the smoke and caress your Energy Field with the smoke. Feel the Cleansing Power of the Smoke as it washes you clean. If you are able, take the Smoke into your lungs and enjoy the sweetness and purity of the cleansing.

Sometimes people with asthma are able to partake of this Sacred Ceremony because for some reason the purity of the

Smoke while being Consecrated as Healing Energy, allows the human body to enter a very different place of awareness. The Sacred Body knows and responds to this good work. When combined with a Medicine Keeper whose Lodge is very pure, and who has lived in high degrees of spiritual dedication, I have seen cases where people with various illnesses have found comfort and even healing of the disease that clings to their bodies. This is not always the case, as everyone's body is different and healing is a very mysterious affair, even in the realms of modern science and medicine. Like many people, I am also not always able to tolerate the Smoke of Ceremony. It depends on the season and issues of general health. Sometimes the best and deepest healing people need and seek internally is a change of heart or mind and this brings along with it internal emotional and spiritual healing and release of burdens.

    If Smoke is difficult, use Water placed in a special bowl. Add a pinch of Salt and say a Blessing over the Water, inviting the Spirit of Water to be present. As you cleanse your body with either Smoke or Water, observe if there is a feeling of release, calm, and/or a sense of freedom. People who cleanse with Sacred Sage say they often feel lighter, as if a weight was lifted from their shoulders. One of our Elders says that spirits and energies attach themselves to our bodies when we pass through the crowd or are with other people whose needs are great. Depending on a person's sensitivity these Energies or Entities can unwittingly become quite a burden to carry around.

    Most people are not aware of this process and so may carry Spirits that are not meant to be carried. This is why daily cleansing is always important, whether with Sacred Smoke, Water, Heat or through what we eat, or how we treat our environment such as by cleaning house, tending the garden, and nourishing the soil. All these activities assist in the cleansing of our bodies, minds, hearts and spirits. But sometimes a cleanse requires clear intention. Not all these activities may generate the result needed if the person is unaware of the underlying process involved.

In this Sacred Snow Blinder Moon, we sit close to the Sacred Fire in this Wigwam remembering the cold weather outside. From the warning of the Frost Fish Moon we know that the Northern hold on the Land and Sea only becomes stronger. There is more winter to come. But even during this Dark Time we know that Spirit is Strong, and the seed of new life lives even through the darkness.

This time of year, we Honour the Turtle, Grandmother of All Tribes of Humanity. She swims down deep into the mud under the lakes to find a place of safety during the freezing times. She alone holds the Keys of Wisdom for our People because her pace is slow, her vision clear, and her ways ensure survival since the beginning of the Creation until now. This is why the original Wigwam was a place of shelter that mirrored the Turtle's shape and size, like the Igloo of our Inuit cousins to the North. We once survived like the Turtle in the deep snows of the last Great Winter (the Ice Age). We survived by digging our way deep into the frozen heart of the Mother. Inside there, we stayed warm and kept watch.

In another part of the world there is Summer and Warmth. As we look to the Southern Door, we pay honour to the Land of Summer and to the Sacred Countries of the South. Being myself very much connected to the Spirits and Dreaming of Australia, I pay honour to the Kangaroo, Dingo and Wedge-tail Eagle who come into my Circle to offer Power and Guidance. You may develop relationships with your Totemic Powers over time. You may want to Honour them with gifts of Tobacco and with the burning of Sage, Cedar and Sweet Grass.

The Four Sacred Herbs of the traditional Mi'kmaq like many things are related to particular Directions and Powers within the Ceremonial Space. Each person, family and tribal group have a different indication of what this means. For example, in the Sacred Ways taught to me, the Energy of Sage works well within the Eastern Door where the Eagle Spirit rises to Teach, Guard, and Protect our work in this lifetime. Eagle is the Messenger who carries our prayers to Creator. Eagle flies highest, and when storm clouds come close, she is the only winged creature that can rise high above the clouds to gain clarity of vision while keeping the connection to the Energy of Light. Sage is associated with this Direction and Power because Sage has the ability to maintain a connection with clarity, vision, insight, warmth and freedom. This allows the Eagle to fly in health and wellbeing.

At this time of the Deep Darkness of the Northern Hemisphere, I remind you that the Mi'kmaq live in a part of the Earth World that sits next to the Northern Inuit Nations. As such, the Power of the North is very strong here. This Power is associated with Turtle Medicine. The Turtle is Mother Earth and represents all of our Grandmothers. A story of the Turtle is shared by the Mi'kmaq. The thirteen squares on the Turtle's back came about when the thirteen tribes of humanity were given birth by the First Mothers who became the Thirteen Grandmothers of humanity. Thus, the Turtle holds all the Ancient Power and Wisdom of Woman's Medicine and Dreaming.

Regardless where you are living when your read these words, you can imagine the Power of the North through its many associations. More sensitive people can actually feel the effects of magnetic energies on their bodies, and literally feel the Power of the North as they travel. Because I have spent two decades of my life under the Southern Stars of Australia, I can now feel the Energy of the North in new ways when I visit Canada. This feels to me a very different energy than the

Southern Pole of the planet which feels more subtle energetically, although to test this theory I would need to visit Tasmania and perhaps travel further South.

Likewise, when I return to Australia my body needs to sit upon Mother Earth and smell the Gum Trees and acknowledge this powerful feeling of drawing toward the Centre of Australia that pulls human energy fields towards Uluru at the Heart of Australia. When I first came to Australia the dominant feeling energetically for me was that I was hanging from the earth by the hairs of my head, because my body was so used to the magnetic poles of the North and was still oriented this way. In the South I felt like I was literally standing on my head.

As my body adjusted, I realised that the Southern Poles change the nature of the Sacred Circle such that the energy flows in a different direction. For several years this process confused and fascinated me. I was uncertain of everything for a while, what the Directions meant, how they worked, what Energies and Powers to honour in each Direction, and how to engage opening and working within the Circle. Then over time the new experience was worked into my sense of spatial awareness and Ceremonial Practice. Eventually I realised the best way for me personally was to honour the Sacred Teachings passed down to me by my Elders, and in this way, I could honour both my traditions as well as honour the Traditional Custodians of the Tribal Country and Nation within which I lived in Australia.

Wherever we live, by honouring these traditions and ways we actually learn over time to be more observing of our bodies. Our connection with land and sea, and the environment around us becomes not just things but actual energies, powerful forces, and moving experiences. We can all relate to the Full Moon in some way, even if only as a pretty object in the sky. But many people associate the Moon in fullness with heightened energy. We can all relate to a thunderstorm. Even if we don't get hit by lightning, we can appreciate the shift of energy in the air and how this makes our bodies feel on edge or excited. This is a magnetic energy and influences our bodies as such.

Thus, you can see by inference that what I am sharing here is much the same. By taking up these practices we learn to be more in-tune with our environment. We form relationships with the land and sea around us. We actually become new Custodians over time because the Original Intention of Creator was to Manifest a People to tend and care for the Earth in each Tribal Nation. The Tribes of Mother Earth are the Original Patchwork Quilt and the Web of Energetic Awareness that Creation manifests to keep the Earth World in Balance. In this way, our Divine Purpose as individuals, families, tribes and nations is to Care for the Earth where we live. Sacred Pipes manifest this web of consciousness among the Custodians.

It should not be surprising that when children are born upon the Earth and when they grow up and have slept upon the Earth for many years, they become a part of the natural environment. They form symbiotic relationships within the environment that include Totemic Powers who come to each person to assist, guide, and teach. Many people are aware of these things even when they do not share the depth of native culture and spirituality. I've heard so many speak of a Crow or an Owl and how the bird appeared at a particular time, giving them a sense of new awareness, a message, or a warning. Many birds appear to remind us of a lost loved one. Others tell us of a coming storm.

These are all experiences of deeper connections with the environment, within the Creation. The advantage of learning these Ways then relates to our being able to live better lives, in greater balance. We can become deeply connected with the land and sea around us. Such that our lives are enriched, made healthier and more fulfilled, and then we rarely feel isolated or alone. We are part of a wider family of relations. We can become deeply connected with the plants, trees, and weather systems; the rocks, hills, valleys and natural features of the land and water bodies; and the winged, finned, four legged, flying and crawling creatures who live and share this Earth World. These connections can teach us many new lessons in life and provide a form of wisdom not readily available to most busy people. We can access wisdom when we allow ourselves to slow down and listen, look, observe, and make our heart and mind open to learning.

Let us again smudge and cleanse our bodies with a small amount of Sacred Sage. Then when we are done, we will light the end of a braid of Sweet Grass. The Sweet Grass is used to honour these Teachings provided today within the Wigwam. We welcome these Teaching and offer Thanks to our Ancestors of all Nations who have provided these insights that connect with our family wisdom traditions. We are reminded that all of us come from tribal roots. All of us on this planet come from an Indigenous land that we would connect with if only we knew where that place was. But because of the teachings we've shared, we also know that if we were born in a place and grew up there, we can still form deep abiding connections with the land and water systems around us. Indeed, all children of Creation are called to become Custodians.

Likewise, if we search deep enough inside ourselves, every person actually carries the energy patterns of the Original Land upon which Creator planted their family heritage even if that was eons ago. Science suggests that human beings evolved from one place on the planet and migrated. This often leaves people feeling disconnected to any place. In contrast, Indigenous teachings from around the world suggest strongly that tribal nations were planted in each location. We grew up as part of the land in that Place. We came to express the spirit and energy of that Land through Song, Dance, Language, and Ceremony. The Spirit of diversity in Creation is expressed through human cultural diversity.

Perhaps both stories have some truth. Migration and being planted in one place. Each location on the planet holds its own Sacred Wisdom teachings. And we are all relations from one family.

Thus when I sit with people from different places, including the descendants of European extraction in Canada, the USA or Australia, and when we explore their family history and begin sharing whatever they might know about their grandparents and beyond, we always tend to come up with many insights about the nature of the Place from which people come. For many this is a profoundly moving experience that leads them to undertake a new journey of reconnecting with their origins, a task that often takes several years to unpack.

I share these experiences only because at this time of the year, during the Snow Blinder Moon, the traditional teachings suggest becoming more aware of our Ancestor's lives is important to our wellbeing. By understanding the challenges and accomplishments they left to us, we can become aware of a part of our own purpose in our generation.

Particularly now, the current generations who are living are given many tasks to resolve prior conflicts that arose in war, illness and hardship as well as poor choices that led to division, relational breakdown, destruction of the environment, and patterns of anger, violence and abuse which includes substance abuse. We are given these tasks by our Ancestors. Our Ancestors are our parents, grandparents, great grandparents and back further through our bloodlines. We ought to remember that time is not relevant when marking the territory in blood. Bloodlines comprise a unique conduit of Energy and Knowledge that we call an innate memory that resides quite often in the Deep

Unconscious, in the World Beneath the Earth, and in the World Beneath the Water. These Places are also Sacred. They also speak to what Carl Jung called the Collective Unconscious as a Place where the combined wisdom teachings of human beings tend to be found.

Reflection

During this New Moon we have shared many new and some familiar teachings. Take time now to leave this shared Wigwam and find your own Space to reflect. Write what stands out to you in your journal. Pick the one, two or three most important ideas or feelings that arise for you. Don't be afraid to mark this book with your favourite pencil or pen. When I love a book you can tell, because I mark that book with little symbols that mean I really like what is said, it stands out for me, I want to remember the idea, the idea needs more research, or I will use that idea to explore in my practice. For each of these kind of insights I have a different form of script or symbol, so when I read the text again it becomes even more familiar to me, and I can easily find what I need when looking for the idea again. You might even note the page of an insight from this book in your journal, so it is easy to find later.

Again, during the growing of the Moon cycle ahead allow yourself to 'keep watch' for any signs or symbolic occurrences in your environment. We have raised the ideas of birds and animal messengers, so it would not surprise me if someone comes to you with a message, whether in daily life or through a dream. When we open up spiritual truths often life changes rather quickly, and new experiences happen because we are ready and have triggered something inside of us that resonates with the world around us. We do live in a profoundly interconnected cosmos. Do not be so surprised if your world expands and becomes influenced by new Energies and Powers who wish to help you.

Likewise, for those of us starting on this journey remember to take it one day at a time. Don't rush too much. Enjoy and be excited, yes. But give things time and don't expect the world to change even if you feel your inner world is changing.

Be wise to the fact that when we open a spiritual doorway, we must be ready to be challenged. The truth is that we may have many hidden fears or anxieties that will come to the surface. This is why most people never want to live a spiritual life. They are afraid. But fear is only given Power by you, no one else.

When we open spiritual pathways, we must be willing to face whatever comes up inside of us. This is given as a profound gift. We need to resolve this challenge before we can move on. That is the way it works. And this is why we are given each other, our Friends, Family, Helpers, Guides, and Powers to assist us. M'sit No'koma, Ta'ho.

Joseph Randolph Bowers

March Siwkewiku's Spawning Moon

Pjila'si ~ Welcome, come in, sit down.

Don't you see, even during the deep darkness new life is growing? This is the time of the great spawning of the Salmon in our rivers and streams. A crisp clarity arises in the mind when we reflect on these mysteries.

Observing Mother Earth is the first form of science. All modern sciences pay tribute to Indigenous Science, because all knowledge and wisdom arises from right observation. When people fail to observe life correctly, that twisted perception leads to harm. Mother Earth has her own logic, patterns, cycles and teachings that lead our People to health and good things.

Those who refuse these teachings do so at their own peril. We see countless examples of this throughout the centuries. Our own People have lived with stories of how greed, pride, anger or jealously claimed the perception of individuals and led to their learning very difficult lessons. Often, they lost their loved ones, their source of living, and their own life – because their decisions were based on incorrect observations of the world around them.

When we are blinded by our internal views, voices or feelings we can easily get sidetracked. But when we observe the world around us and listen, really listen and stay open to learning, we will find the path of wisdom left for us by our Elders, by the Teachers of Mother Earth. These teachers are all of our relations in the Winged, Finned, Four Legged, Crawling and Leafy creatures who inhabit the Land and Sea. Each are our Teacher, Brother and Sister, Mother, Father and Grandparents. Only with blind pride do people forget these important truths. Then in pride and arrogance, people proceed down a path of destruction.

Like most of my Mi'kmaq cousins we have embraced the newcomers since the 17th century. I can trace my family heritage back to 1652 in Mi'kma'ki, when our French Acadian Ancestor Michel Richard married a Mi'kmaw bride. This history is documented and held in trust by the Mi'kmaq Resource Centre at Cape Breton University, which is a repository of information by and about the Mi'kmaq Nation, held in trust for the Chiefs and Elders of the Nation.

For this reason, I can say with some certainty that the European tribes lost their way when they began to perceive that human beings are separate from Mother Nature. With the rise of colonial powers through the conquests of Greece, Rome and the Christian Empire, subsequent generations of European tribes began to internalise the myth of separation and domination of the Earth. These movements continued and culminated in the Industrial Revolution, after which time even the spiritual nature of life was separated from commerce and economics. This led to the wholesale denial of ecologically balanced values. It is no wonder that during these years even children were used and abused in the factories of Europe. What a sad legacy for modern people that all of our major industrial advances were built on the blood and backs of children. But alas, this is only one of the legacies of the European tribe's greater mistakes.

To some extent, most of the advances of the modern world can be traced back to the imbalances and errors of perception within the European story. European colonial history is long and complex. We know that conquests of European tribes date back over one hundred thousand years, back to a time when Europe was made up of numerous matriarchal tribes who honoured the earth as Mother. The early influences of patriarchal tribes from the north into Europe combined with the empirical advances of Greek, Roman and later, Christian domination.

Since at least the Middle Ages the Roman Catholic Church held great power surpassed only by the rise of monarchy and more recently the social and political power of centralised governments. We cannot forget the huge influence of western intellectual movements since the enlightenment era leading to the rise of science, and during the last two centuries, the emerging culture of empirical secularism. Most of these beliefs have side stepped the Indigenous wisdom of countless tribes across Europe. What might seem like harmless modern movements like humanism and existentialism can be traced to early colonial efforts to subdue and incorporate Indigenous tribal knowledge in North America, Australia, New Zealand and in many other colonial nations. Much of present-day professional discourse, theory and academic work relies heavily on these origins, and moving toward an authentic post-colonial culture may take another few decades at best.

But the post-colonial movement, especially among Indigenous scholars, provides some hope for transforming culture. In my efforts over the past two decades, the importance of finding balance is centre stage. In many ways the European story inherited by Australia, Canada, the USA and New Zealand gives rise to extremes of beliefs and values that do harm to sustainable ways of living. Indigenous scholarship points toward a middle ground where the Sacred and the Secular can meet within a rather logical and creative approach to science, knowledge and spirituality.

As a basis, Indigenous traditions teach about the importance of right perception and holding sacred the ordinary events and happenings of each day. By acknowledging the sacred we have built into our way of life a system of values and beliefs that honour the environment around us. Only the modern world thinks that the sacred is the opposite of the secular and equates the secular with science, truth and knowledge. This separation again goes back to how the western Christian Church dominated people's lives to such a degree that this modern illusion about the sacred verses the secular remains a part of the post-trauma recovery of whole societies. We have a choice. We do not have to follow in this history of unbalanced perceptions of nature and spirituality.

Colonial histories have led to great imbalances of ethical and moral values that have eroded people's relationships with local, regional and national ecosystems. Loss of what we might consider as traditional Indigenous cultural values has allowed communities and societies to dominate and abuse the land and to exploit its natural resources. These issues have consistently led to the extinction and genocide of hundreds and thousands of species around the world. Human societies continue to impose constraints and unjust laws upon other human societies. Threats to cultural diversity combine with ecological harm, resulting in less access to important knowledge and wisdom - leaving all human beings more vulnerable.

These histories separated people from nature. And the central challenge of the post-modern days we live in relate to bringing people back to nature, and nature back to people. We are one. Though we are many. When we walk back in time past the artificial divisions of the western tribes, back through all the days of the Christian dispensation, back further we find a deeper tribal wisdom that still lies hidden in the psyche of every person. When we look even deeper, we find within the Song Lines of All Nations an Ecological Wisdom we can connect with here, in this simple Wigwam.

No habit of thought has the power to divide and separate forever. Human beings are isolated from Mother Earth only because of these phantoms, these habits of thought that are false perceptions. To 'isolate' means to 'separate equals.' We are equal with All Our Relations in Creation. We cannot remain isolated, because we are One in Being. One in Truth. One in Substance.

There is but One Fire at the Heart of Mother Earth. There is One Sun who gives us life and who feeds all plants, animals and peoples. There is but One Grandmother Moon who lights the night sky, bringing balance and harmony to the lakes, rivers and oceans. She it is who governs the Spirits of the Deep Waters. There is but One Song of Creation, with many Languages, upon Countless Aboriginal Lands where Creator Planted a People.

So, during this Sacred Moon we remember this Ancient Wisdom. We know in our hearts and minds this wisdom holds the key to unlock the divisions of today's world. We know that we are sons and daughters of the Creator, and that we are called to manifest today the Power of the First Medicines. These teachings arise at this time for a specific purpose. Each person will know why and how. Listen to your heart. Observe the world around you, and you will see the truth.

During this New Moon time, ask your God or Goddess for a sign of what new things are to come in your lifetime? Ask for a manifestation of some spiritual truth. Then wait. Be patient. When we seek the Elders, we are told to be patient... We know that in fact no answer will usually come back right away. Elders tend to take their time and come back when they are ready. There is no obligation to even answer the specific question asked in some literal way. Elders often take things to heart and they pray. They wait for insights that are meant to be passed on to us younger ones.

So, when we ask God for a sign, an answer, or a manifestation of some vision or dream or hope – we must also be patient. And we ought to remember that God is a lot like our Elders. The Creator is a community of being, a Sacred Entity of at least Three Persons in One. The Creator has taken millions of years to Create with Love all that we know. Every strand of the Great Web is a part of the greater Mystery of Life – and every moment is an Unfolding Mystery. Why do we make ourselves so important that we feel the Creator of All might even hear our prayer, let alone come to answer us swiftly on our schedule and in our calendar? It seems highly unlikely.

And yet the very substance of Creation leans toward giving us whatever we wish for when those wishes are well aligned with the Original Teachings. If what we seek is good, whole, balanced and in harmony; and when we seek with our hearts in sync with our minds; often we will receive our answer even if that takes some time or even a few years.

So be careful what you ask for. You are more likely to receive than not. And when you do, it may not be what you expected, and may demand much of you that you never realised before. With every spiritual gift comes a responsibility. Quite often spiritual gifts come with something we must let go of that we never expected, and it can be extremely difficult. Life is like this sometimes. We must be tested and grow into who we are becoming.

Reflection

We take this Moon time to remember. Ask God to fulfil your life purpose. As the Moon moves to fullness, write in your journal any insights that arise. Observe your world and wait for a sign. Be active yourself and make things move forward as you can – God does not want an idle servant. Pray as if everything depends on you, and act as if everything depends on God. If you take things this way, you will only pray for what is true to your inner being. God will honour that kind of honesty. God will very likely open up much more than you ever expected. From little things big things grow. God will take your prayers and offer much more in return.

When you act as if everything depends on Creator, you will be walking in humility. Your Higher Power will honour your truth of heart. If you depend on God, you will walk in confidence. Your inner life will grow. You will become stronger. Your inner strength will be based not in your ego, or your personal efforts. Your identity will become based on something much more Powerful, Energetic and Vital.

By taking these attitudes you will begin a process of becoming a Custodian of your own Path in Life. This will open up Spiritual Power that moves in sync with the Original Teachings. Greater things come to those who wait and are humble of heart. M'sit No'koma. Ta'ho.

Sacred Teachings

Siwkw/Spring Moons

April Penatemuiku's Egg Laying Moon

Pjila'si ~ Welcome, come in, sit down.

During the dark new moon, we sit and talk, listen and wait. We look into the flames of the Sacred Fire. What do you see there, hidden in the Great Mystery of the Flames coming to Life?

Indeed, Life is Sacred and is all around us. We know from ages past that the energy of the Flames is the same as the energy from the Sacred Stars. How did our Ancestors know this? They taught that we are made from the Sacred Dust of the Stars. Our bodies return to that from which we were first made. In what manner did our Elders see, hear or touch this profoundly simple yet spiritual knowledge?

While you stare into the Flames of Life, be aware of your body. Allow your mind to become restive. With each in-breath take in the Sacred smells of Sweet Grass and Sage burning ever so slowly beside the Fire. Our Wigwam is the Place of Family. The hearth of Comfort, Safety and Assurance. We are the Stars that Sing. We are People of the Dawn. Our Light Shines forth in the Great Expanse of Darkness. We see our Totem Spirits moving across the Star World, the Pathway of the Ancients.

In the Flames imagine you see your Life as it is now. Imagine you are watching your own Life unfold from the Place of the Stars. Imagine your awareness is able to Fly with Sparrow and take on the clear sight of the Eagle. Look into your unfolding Life and watch as your Life evolves, changes, and grows.

Take a few deep breaths. Breathe deeply and let your tensions go... Let them be burned up in the Flames of Sacred Unfolding. When you are ready, allow the pictures and images to reveal to you something Sacred about your Life Path. Allow the Speaking Flames to Sing Your Life back into Balance and Beauty. Look for what you Need - what your inner heart truly desires. Look for that something that lies outside of your awareness, beyond your fondest dreams, outside of your conscious cravings. Allow the Eagle's Eye to show you in the Flames of Dancing your True and Sacred Purpose in Life.

Some say they see their children's faces. Other see their future in clarity and truth. Many see their own reflection and are horrified. Some are drawn deeper into the flames to such a degree that their physical bodies may fall forward. But we Elders are waiting, and we hold these ones back to protect them from falling into the Flames. But we know inwardly they continue to fall. They ride the Wings of the Eagle into the Sacred Fire at the Heart of Mother Earth. We who have taken that pathway know the dangers of the World Beneath the Earth. Of primary concern is for those who are not prepared to see their own reflection in the Flames. Truth is sometimes hard to bear.

One person from the World Beneath the Earth told me that they saw an Empty Hand. They were transfixed. They did not know what to think. This Sacred Hand was old and worn, tired and strong. As they described the Hand my heart sank with wonder... Could it be? They did not know the fate that lay before them and what this vision meant to their future. In my heart I sat in wonder, and burned more Sage before the Fire...

Some of us are given to the most profound purpose of all. We are called and propelled by our genes, our inner nature. Our hearts were given to us by Creator before we were born. We are impelled into the Sacred Flames of Life to give everything we are to others in loving kindness. Our path in life is set even before we breathe air. We are given to our Mothers and Fathers, Sisters and Brothers, before we enter the world of Flesh while our Sacred Drumbeats still in that Realm beyond the Womb.

It is in this Place of Wonder that my heart weeps the most. When I look upon the Face of a Child, and I know the cosmic potential and Sacred Power that rests in every human heart. The energy we carry is idle no more. We are awakened to Flames Dancing. Our pathwork is a Sacred Art. Others may see what we do as political action, even as selfish and short sighted. But they do not know the Fire that Burns.

For the Mi'kmaq People who have literally and figuratively carried the Fire that Burns for hundreds of thousands of years, we know that when the Spirit Eye of Eagle awakens our awareness, our Life is made Sacred. We are changed. Our future actions are given to us. We are moved by the Stars who Sing. We are in touch with the Passion and Power of our Ancestors.

In the simplicity of this, we know we are a People given to humanity by the Sacred Dawn. Our lives are not our own. We are born to a Purpose.

Reflection

Record in your journal what you saw in the flames, or what your experience was like. If you like, draw or paint, crochet or use natural elements from the environment around you to make something that reflects the experience. If you have not started with a Medicine Bundle, consider asking Creator for a Sacred Object from your world to speak to you a special message about this time in your life. Record your request in your journal, and playfully wait to see how long it takes for that prayer to be answered. We cannot force a gift from Creator. But we do know that Creator wants to give us things that are helpful to our spiritual and human growth. The gift may come across your path, or someone may give you something. It will be fascinating to see what happens and what meaning you find in that gift. M'sit No'koma. Ta'ho.

Sacred Teachings

May Etqoljewiku's Frog-Croaking Moon

Pjila'si ~ Welcome, come in, sit down.

For many Moons I have sat under the Southern Door, watching the Stars who Sing. In my sitting, the Eagle Medicine Pipe often rests in my hands. Often, I see the northern hemisphere and the Great Lands of the Northern Peoples across Turtle Island. The Dark Land is before me and looks like an expanse of Stars.

Once I asked Great Spirit, who are these Stars who Sing? The answer came to me only after several more Moons of Sitting. Slowly the awareness came through a series of visions and dreams.

Joseph Randolph Bowers

In one dream the Land was dying, I mean really dying. There were beings I could only see as evil embodied who were making decisions over the Land that caused enormous suffering to Mother Earth. In my dream She awoke with great pain. Her insides where being torn apart. She screamed and I woke up in a start. My body was tense and sweaty, the beads pouring from my face.

In another dream the Land was already dead. She looked like the face of the Moon. No plants or animals grew there anymore. That dream was a haunting that stays with me and causes me to sit and pray.

In another vision before the Fire I saw a small child. She was laughing and hugging her father. Her face was radiant and beautiful, innocent and pure. Then I was shown an Elder with wrinkled face and tinkling eyes of brown. He was sitting with a Sacred Pipe. The Smoke was healing and moving and flowed from my vision into my heart. In that feeling was a kind of inner strength borne of many battles. Tears flowed from my eyes as my heart was moved by the Elder's strength and silence.

Still other visions came to me while sitting by the Fire. Of a sapling being born beneath the soils of the Sacred Tundra in North Eastern Quebec. Of a White Buffalo Calf coming forth from her Mother's womb. Of a Salmon jumping through the waters of a river along the Eastern Shore of Nova Scotia, moving toward her spawning grounds once again. Of a Women ripe with child, sitting over a wooden table looking into the small flame of a candle. She had sadness in her eyes, and from that sadness I saw her man far out to sea in a fishing vessel. He was pushing against the wind. She was pulling his spirit close to her.

These and many other intuitive sights led me to wonder even more. What are the Lights I see when I look upon the Northern Door of Turtle Island? It was given then in my heart that the Stars before me were Pure Moments of Truth in the Heart of Creation. It was then I finally understood.

Great Spirit came over me and said, 'The Light of Life you see is the very Pulse of the Land. She needs this Purity and Loving Kindness. She is tired and worn out. Mother Earth is suffering and grows weary of her children who no longer show respect. *She shows you the Children of Pure Heart. She shows you the path back to balance and beauty. She shows you the path back to truth and justice for the Land and Sea. Watch and listen to the Stars who Sing.*' In humility my face was cast down. How can I ever live up to this calling, Great Spirit? How can I ever walk this path of purity in heart, when all about me such a complex world distracts me every day?

Then a sadness like the heavy feeling before a great storm came over my life and covered me with a blanket of sorrow. In the darkness there were no longer any Lights whatsoever. The Land was raped bare and left like a waste. Scars were torn all over her. Whole mountains were laid low, and by no means under a sacred intention. Rivers were polluted and lakes dead with purple slime and dark oil lapping at dead animals and fish. People were starving all across the Great North, dying from cold with no wood to burn in their fires. And in this vast sea of sadness the small remaining Lights were only those of a few Elders and young children still untouched by the Dark Spirit of Greed. But that was all that remained.

Hidden were all the Sacred Pipes of the Nations. Dark were all the Fire Pits of the Sacred Arts. In mourning were the Elders. Hiding in fear and protected by their parents were the few remaining young children, even more rare in this time of suffering. Humanity was on the very brink of disaster and no longer carried the resilience of the Ages past. And so, few it was who had any awakening to the Life of Truth, the Land Herself lay lifeless and forlorn.

Great Spirit then spoke to me. 'Listen carefully. I will say this but once. There is a reason my People of the Dawn are called to Ceremony and Life. One and the same. Life and Ceremony. To be the conscience of humanity is no small task. The Medicines are Sacred because they Give Life. People must walk the Sacred Way to understand. You are the Spirit of the Child, the Mother, the Elder. You are called to be Sacred. To Protect and Guard the Sacred Doors.'

Only very slowly did my vision return. I had been blinded by these Words of Light. By early morning my body was stiff, tired and weary. In my vision there were Stars once again. Images like phantoms came to me. Small children having fun in the clearing of a forest. Elders drinking tea by the fire. Wolf packs playing and foraging in the woods. And warnings of conflicts in blockades, protests, signs being photographed and shared around the world. Faces of people concerned for justice. Hunger fasting by people of conscience pulled to the limits of their spiritual strength...

It was then that I finally understood. If we do not awaken to the Spiritual Medicines, we will make the Mother suffer and die a very painful death. If we refuse to acknowledge the Truth that Lives all around us, we risk a form of blind ignorance that must surely have inspired the first invaders to cut down the thousand-year-Old Growth Forests of North America to build larger and stronger ships for the empire. Those ships were sunk eons ago. The forests are still gone. No one bothered to replant. No one bothers to give back to Mother Earth. It would take at least five hundred years to see the first generation of an Old Growth Forest of that scope and majesty as once existed in Eastern Canada and the New England States of the USA. Now that is a worthy project for our generation.

Stupidity leads to fracturing the Earth for monetary gains. But ten or twenty years of profit is not enough to warrant the destruction of an ecosystem for a thousand years. Present day government leaders insist they know what is right. But their face is formed of Darkness. Their eyes are mad from Blindness. Their words and deeds carry violence to the Earth and her Peoples. Ironic that we who live in Fourth World conditions still stand up as the conscience of society in Canada, the USA, Australia, New Zealand, and so many other countries around the world.

Through the past fourteen generations of suffering we have learned as a Nation to remain focused on the Light of Truth. Our philosophy is linked to the Land and Sea. Our Native Way is very Strong and full of Power. The Red Road is filled with integrity, honour and respect.

Reflection

Imagine you too are a small Light, a Sacred Star in the expanse of night. What does your Star Sing? What music do you buzz into the world? Use your imagination and creativity. Express the energy, colour, flavour, or sounds of your Life-Force.

As you play with this experience, know that your Life-Force is as simple as your breathing. You are Alive. You have Purpose in your Existence. You are a Child of the Stars. Your Ancestors are watching over you. Your Angels hover around you. Listen to their Energy and Power. They hold many messages of love, guidance and protection for your path.

As you begin to walk the Sacred Path, remember the world around you. Remember the environment, the trees, animals and plants in your local ecosystem. What can you do to protect and nurture them? What sacrifice are you willing to give to protect these Sacred Relations in your world? What can you do in the process of changing lifestyles and approaches to consumption, to purchasing, and to using items that come from natural resources?

Joseph Randolph Bowers

Native spirituality is deeply practical. How can your life change to become more in-tune with the natural world? What can you give back to Mother Earth each day? M'sit No'koma. Ta'ho.

June Nipniku's Summer Moon

Pjila'si ~ Welcome, come in, sit down.

Healing from trauma means many things. In my work as a counsellor and psychotherapist, counsellor educator, and natural healer who remembers and acknowledges Indigenous forms of healing and insight, trauma can become a deep part of our identity. The parts of us that are hurting and that remember trauma need our help.

Sacred Teachings

We naturally resist parts of ourselves (and parts of our families) that are hurting. It is easy to push away a hurting part. In the European traditions of conquest, colonisation, and being conquered and dominated, families learned, and internalised denial of the pains caused by selfish motivation. Mainstream economics push away the reality of hurt caused by so-called progress. The hurts of our Aboriginal peoples caused by colonisation and today's selfish materialism are also forgotten by our white and mainstream brothers and sisters.

In a way then, how people push away hurt makes those of us who are hurting feel more alone. Splinter politics is a form of pushing each other away. We divide against each other in our Nation to our own demise. Youth suicide is one big example of how people get to be isolated and how everyone loses so much by not standing together in solidarity in our pain, trauma, and struggles for a better life. Sometimes all we need is to listen to each other's stories, to hear and feel the hurt that is never spoken… then we can learn how to reach out and help each other more.

So, this story has many parts. There is the big story – the macro story of cultures, peoples, and histories. Then there is the little story – our story, the story of our families and our personal stories. All of these stories have Medicine for us, if we are willing to listen.

If we listen long enough and can endure the pain of each other's trauma stories, something beautiful happens. For me this happened powerfully when I began to listen to the trauma stories of my Aboriginal friends and family in Australia. Even though I come from Nova Scotia and honour my Mi'kmaw heritage through my father and grandmother who taught me a quiet pride and appreciation for who we are, I never understood the story of colonisation in all of its power, horror, and pain until I came to Australia.

It was through listening to the stories in another tribal country that the pain in my own family history came up within me – my heart, soul, and spirit remembered, and the pain was re-awakened. This process put me in shock for several years. Over the first ten years I had been in Australia shock turned to my own trauma recovery, and in this came a deepening resolve to work in healing and to assist people to move from trauma to empowerment.

Healing from trauma can have really intense times, like seasons, or periods of years, and then can kind of rest easy for a while, but always seems to come back to tell another tale. Trauma stories do change over time, because if we listen openly, we really do learn from our trauma. But this process isn't easy. No way.

The flip side is that healing from trauma gives many new seeds for spring growth. But the secret is that you have to live through the winter. Trauma is a bitter kind of winter in the underworld, maybe somewhere between the spirit world and the underworld where people's spirits are caught betwixt and between.

We do lose a part of ourselves when we live through extreme forms of trauma – and the recovery of a lifetime can be so difficult for us and for our families. But in my experience of working with many people in healing, to get somewhere new you have to live through the pain – you have to be where you are right now before you can move forward. Humans cannot push it aside or down; it only gets locked up in the body and causes more harm. Trauma needs to be acknowledged, mourned, felt and shared in stories and songs. The healing from our trauma is the strength of our Nation.

Professor Judy Atkinson is an Australian Aboriginal woman of great wisdom and I look to her as an esteemed elder. She wrote a powerful book called *Trauma Trails: Recreating Song*

Lines. Look her up by doing a Google on the internet. She teaches that trauma is intergenerational – our trauma is often passed down from generation to generation. Nothing new to Mi'kmaq People's wisdom, where we know seven generations are always the minimum number to be deeply interconnected.

But likewise, healing is also intergenerational. I can remember during fasting and prayer seeing a Great Grandmother in traditional dress, she was weeping and singing out to her grandchildren generations down the line. When it hit me, she might be singing to me so one day we might wake up and remember who we are – my life was changed forever. My heart sank and tears rolled for several hours, rocking back and forth my pain and sorrow, love and caring, piecing together the broken fragments of our history, our story, our medicine. Several years later I discovered some of my cousins were on the Red Road of Mi'kmaw spirituality and in our own way, we each are putting the puzzle back together.

Healing surely goes across the generations, probably even more than pain and trauma. I believe this is true because we always tend to overlook the goodness in life. We take things for granted. What is your choice? Will you take up the healing path for yourself and your children? Will you deal with your pain and trauma now? Or pass this on through silence to your children's children? Knowing that healing happens when we open our hearts, this gives me peace and connection to Mother Earth regardless where life puts me. I wish you to heal and strength in your Spirit, Heart, and Body. If you let your mind follow the wisdom of these Three Sacred Energies, the walls will start to crumble down. New paths will open up. Just listen to your inner voice – Eagle Medicine is not far off.

Reflection

The reflection during this moon time may open up many old energies, memories or associations - so please be gentle, kind and compassionate with yourself. Only go there if you feel strong enough. And don't push. If you wish to enter into that pathway of healing self-reflection on your own trauma story, or your unresolved issues, take it slow and one step at a time.

Otherwise, just take some time off and enjoy the moment. Focus on something playful and joyful. Enjoy your kids. Watch a movie. Go for a walk in your favourite place in nature. Watch the waves of the ocean if you live close by. Or make it a point to get up early and watch the Sacred Sunrise. You may also decide to be part of a Sacred Sun Set.

Either way, be aware of intentionally becoming more aware of the world around you. By building this relationship you are taking the first small steps in a 'round about healing' approach. Healing can be heaps of fun when we do things this way. Healing by directly focusing on an issue, problem or past hurt can often backfire. It leads us into the whole complex of feelings and despair associated with being overwhelmed.

But shifting the focus onto fun and lovely things is a Sacred Mystery found in the Old Ways of the People - of how the human heart can heal by just thinking a lovely thought. Turn your mind and heart to things that mean the most to you. And enjoy bringing more goodness into your life. M'sit No'koma. Ta'ho.

Sacred Teachings

Nipk/Summer Moons

July Peskewiku's Feather-shedding Moon

Pjila'si ~ Welcome, come in, sit down.

Last month we discussed healing from trauma and flowing from that comes insight about working with trauma memories. Let me suggest from the beginning that this article may increase people's awareness of issues that you might carry such as trauma.

If you are not ready for this, skip reading this article for now and put it aside for a time when you really feel prepared. Everything has its time. There is no shame in this.

Here are a few key suggestions to help in the meantime. Read the rest of the article later on down the track.

Make sure you have a support system in place. Find out where to access counselling. Let your friend or family member know about your courageous steps forward. When you really feel ready, read the rest of the article below.

First off, let me explain some basic information about trauma.

Trauma experiences generate many responses, and it is helpful to understand these so that (1) we do not feel like total freaks and (2) we can realise our experience is actually pretty normal. By doing this, we can eventually become friends with our trauma-burden, the part of us that was impacted, abused, or violated in some way.

There are many forms of trauma of course, and to respect this diversity my comments may apply to some folk's experiences but not to others. So, I always say, take what is helpful for you and disregard the rest.

Also, while I try to speak in general terms, trauma is not general – it is always deeply personal.

So, for those of us trying to understand our loved one's experience, we need to be really open-minded. We need to keep our hearts ready for feeling empathy. Empathy is a way of standing with someone when you may not have experienced the same things, but still you stand in support and let your loved one know in many ways you are there for them.

Trauma is first experienced by many people as shock, horror, and dismay.

Sometimes trauma occurs very early in people's lives, in their childhood. Aboriginal people who endured separation from their families and who survived the residential schools may carry deeply embedded trauma memories from their school years. In a way, the longer people carry trauma memories the more deeply embedded in memory these experiences are. The longer we tend to carry trauma, the more this may influence our sense of self and our identity. On one hand, we may always carry the loss and forms of grief this implies, even if this may change in certain ways over time. On the other hand, we may grow stronger, and some people may even transform their lives and identity long after the past trauma experience.

Other forms of trauma happen as an adult, such as having a car accident or surviving a fire. Another form of trauma is ongoing or chronic. There are many forms of chronic trauma, such as continual physical pain, emotional turmoil, financial stress, unemployment, and social forms of trauma caused by racism, violence, and the many results of substance abuse.

Addiction to substances and other forms of addiction can be experienced as causing trauma and as traumatic in their own right. But here again, each person's experience might be different – so we keep our minds open to learn from each person what their story reveals.

After the initial shock of trauma, various processes kick in. Physically the human body may actually go into shock. This process can take hours or days, and even weeks to unfold and resolve.

We need to understand that our state, whatever it is, will pass into some new experience.

Usually after extreme trauma the experience will improve – but the person's awareness will actually expand and deepen. This increasing awareness and revisiting the trauma experience may actually make things harder, not easier.

In past I have worked with war veterans whose trauma memories were quite acute. Likewise, many women who have memories of rape, incest, and family violence carry extremely difficult memories. Often memories will resurface in people's dreams and waking moments for unknown reasons. By being unknown, the person's memories may also carry feelings of panic, dismay, uncertainty, fear, and anxiety related to having the memory in the now. This is all normal and part of natural healing processes.

Often clients find these processes really upsetting, largely because of the uncertainty involved in worry that the difficult experience of memories is unhealthy, a sign of sickness, or a bit crazy. Just coming to terms with how normal the process of healing can be is a big part of the healing itself. We already suffered enough! We don't need to make ourselves suffer more in fear and anxiety. Embracing our healing is a wonderful opportunity for the trauma-laden person, and for their family members. Our children and youth need to learn about healing as a natural way, a path through life. This will help them when they need hope for the future.

So many people have come to me because their experiences of having memories of trauma are so disconcerting that their daily lives are being disrupted. Many of these cases are people in their adult to elder years, who later in life experience more memory of their trauma not less.

These experiences are quite normal. Indeed, they appear quite common among trauma recovery cases.

Memories resurface from the hurting part of us because that part needs our help or wishes to tell us something helpful. When we actually accept this as a possibility, we can learn to dialogue with our hurting part – to listen to the story of this part of us that was traumatised in the past. By doing this in various ways, we come to terms with the powerlessness and sometimes desperation we might have felt under the circumstances.

From this realisation many clients come to another even more powerful realisation of how amazing and wonderful their inner self really is – because they not only survived the trauma experience, but their mind and heart protected them from total self-destruction. In reality human beings (and especially children and youth) can endure such extremes of trauma precisely because of how the human body protects us from further harm through the innate trauma response. This response relates to the nature of 'shock.'

Shock is an amazing gift of Creator. In the human body shock is a protector, a shield. Shock is like the Shieldwolf who goes ahead of the pack to make sure everything is safe. Then this alpha wolf will get the signal, everything is safe, and will lead the rest of the pack forward. Shock is the part of our bodies and spirits that goes ahead. If things are not safe, that part kicks in and shields the rest of our inner world from danger.

In this way, shock removes the full weight of trauma from our minds and allows us to survive. Only later in life are we strong enough to face the full realisation of the trauma. So, for folks who have mid-life or later-life awakenings, from my point of view this is completely normal.

In some ways people grow stronger in spite of their crisis. Over time people do tend to heal. Often this happens in ways that seem totally unrelated to the trauma – like how people move on to create new lives, or learn new skills, or just focus on something different. Often, we choose to take up the healing path to help other people in similar circumstances – healing is a sacred circle.

Sometimes those of us who are called to the healing path will actually get sick ourselves unless we reach out in healing to others. These gifted souls tell all of us a huge but simple teaching. Human beings naturally move towards healing. We do this because we naturally want to be healthy, well, balanced, and caring spirits.

We live in our sacred drums with skin stretched over us. We might fool ourselves to think we are alone, isolated, and worthless. But we only fool ourselves. Great Spirit knows who we are and waits for us to awaken. When only one star goes into super nova, the whole universe shivers and awakens that little bit more. When one human spirit wakes from sleep, every part of creation shivers, sings, and dances.

So, when it comes to trauma memories, every little growth and tiny healing counts. These experiences of growth help us move toward awakening the whole self. Oddly, when many of us get there we don't even realise it because it just feels natural. One day we might remember our past trauma, now or in a future time, and we are surprised that we feel strong enough to remember without being so overwhelmed.

There is much hope. Trauma does dissipate over time, and people can move on through remembering. But the mainstream idea of pushing pain aside and getting on with life is actually just repeating the trauma cycle. The best ways to break the cycle are to acknowledge whatever we feel, to engage in cultural ritual, to share stories as medicine, and to accept each other's pain – by embracing our humanity we become who we are meant to be.

Reflection

During the New Moon, if you decided not to engage the reflection on trauma, I suggest you continue the journey offered during the last moon time. That is, to concentrate on things lovely and beautiful that you can enjoy and celebrate in life. Consider doing a craft, making a Dream Catcher, collecting small stones and making a symbolic Sacred Circle where you can grow flowers or collect special items. Your imagination is the only limitation. Remember the world around you and ground your efforts in building a stronger and more resourceful relationship with your local ecology.

If you have engaged the trauma and healing reflection, you can take many different pathways during your New Moon. One pathway might be to become more aware of ways you can heal and move forward with your life. This pathway is about personal growth and wellness. Another pathway might be to consider how you can help others to feel better about themselves. This pathway is about social and familial growth and wellness. Often these two paths overlap. Your growth may be tied in with helping other people. Remember that in giving we receive much more. In offering to others, we step outside of our personal limited views and experiences. We may even learn something by reaching out. M'sit No'koma. Ta'ho.

Joseph Randolph Bowers

August Peskewiku's Feather-shedding Moon

Pjila'si ~ Welcome, come in, sit down.

Last month we explored working with traumatic memories. This article changes the focus to empowerment through reclaiming personal space.
Often when I am working with people who have experienced some form of human violation, like violence, crime, rape, incest, family abuse, or financial manipulation, part of the work that is most helpful involves reclaiming personal space. We begin with a very simple exercise.
Stand somewhere with lots of space around your body, enough to swing your arms around without touching anything.

Flex your knees and take a deep breath. Breathe into your tension and let it out with your exhale. Do this a few times. Then lift your arms and circle around your body by extending the tips of your fingers as far from your body as you can comfortably reach.

As you turn around, be aware that this is your own personal space. This is the space given to you by Creator, by your God, whatever name you give him or her. This space is your own sacred circle, your place of safe harbour from the rest of the world. This space is unique to you, because no one else has it, and no one else can share it unless you let them into your space physically.

I then ask people to become aware of how this space feels, and to remember a time when they were feeling very in-tune with Creator or Creation, some place perhaps by the ocean or in the woods, where they felt completely at one with their life and energy.

Most people remember such a time easily. Some find it a great challenge if they are dealing with depression or very low energy. These folks might remember the time but cannot access the powerful feelings and energy as much. Whatever your experience, the point is to honour and respect whatever you feel. There is no right or wrong.

There is a great insight here. Even for people who only remember hard times and down times, this experience itself is very powerful. I ask the person to be aware of how they are feeling, and how this influences their personal space around their body. I let them know that darker feelings are just as powerful as lighter feelings – and just as worthy of our attention and increasing awareness. All our feelings have important information to tell us, and we can be curious what they want to tell us as we explore our sacred circle.

Now I suggest the person takes the tips of their fingers and draws an imaginary circle around their body on the floor or ground around them. Sometimes clients will pick things from my office to use to mark the circle. Other times when we are in nature, folks will mark the circle with sticks or stones that are around.

Once the person has their circle well defined, I ask them to stand or sit, and just to enjoy the thought that this is their own special sacred space. This is the place of their personal power – to make choices in their life, and to consider the people in their life.

From here we begin to imagine their life in new ways. Together with me as a special companion on their journey, clients share their stories of pain, loss, grief, or excitement, newness, and anticipation.

This process may lead me to suggest awareness of the seven sacred directions, bringing into the circle the wisdom of Native traditions that echo the major world religions and many other Aboriginal traditions across the world. For example, the circle is parallel to the Christian sanctuary formed by the cross with its four directions, and the altar forming directions of above, below, and centre – a place of personal awareness and spiritual transformation. The seven directions parallel the seven Christian sacraments. Aboriginal traditions far out date other world religions and connect us with our deeper indigenous human and ecological roots.

Because the directions take in all our relations, whatever decisions we contemplate in this personal space will tend to be ethical and wholistic. We consider how our decision will impact other people, and we seek guidance from our higher power – by whatever name we give that being.

However, people integrate this experiential learning into their own beliefs and cultural values, mostly all people I have taught realise how important and empowering the experience can be. For instance, Chinese people tell me how the learning brought them back to their spiritual traditions in a contemporary way that made sense for them, and Aboriginal Australian people share similar insights that brought them back to their Dreamtime Serpent and local Dreaming stories.

Clients often take these experiences and insights and explore them on their own. Once you know the process you can go there anytime, do the work you need to do, gain some new awareness, reclaim your space for yourself, and redirect your future according to the insight you gain in your sacred circle.

Sometimes people tell me they realised they were simply meant to accept their life as it has been, and to change their attitude in some basic way to make things easier. Other times people move their lives in many new directions. Either way, I admire people's courage and insight when they are able to listen to their inner voice. In today's world these traditional ways are to be greatly admired.

Thus, in teaching these basic processes of personal awareness to people from all different religions, cultures, and countries, in Canada, America, Australia, Europe, and Hong Kong, wherever I go people are excited to learn about the underlying principles of empowerment, awareness, ethics, and justice that are so deeply embedded in our First Nation Canadian traditions.

The point is that these processes work. The world is seeking help and our own people are looking for answers – but truth is, we already have the answers inside our own traditions. Our First Nation heritage is a wealth of empowerment for those of us who are ready and willing to take some risks, to reclaim our space, and move forward with life.

Reflection

During this New Moon consider recording your adventure with opening a circle and finding your personal space, defining that space, and coming to terms with your life in new ways.

What have you decided to reclaim in your life? What good feeling do you want to see increase? What personal boundaries would you like to respect more and more? Open to the possible.

As you explore these experiences, do a bit of research into your familial and cultural traditions. Look for any signs of the Old Ways in your cultural heritage. What expressions of the basic principles of personal empowerment, ceremony and self-awareness can you find?

What new traditions would you like to share with your children, and your grandchildren? Remember that you are in a place where you have the power to redefine the meaning of your life. This can come to help your children and their children for years to come. Give this some serious thought and prayerful consideration. M'sit No'koma. Ta'ho.

Sacred Teachings

September Wikumkewiku's Moose-calling Moon

Pjila'si ~ Welcome, come in, sit down.

Last month we explored reclaiming personal space. During this month of autumn when we are preparing for the winter to come, and gearing up for the new season, I am reminded of ways we can work in sacred space and bring new balance into the world. In this wigwam where we sit together, we are sharing many insights. Thank you for visiting with me. Thank you for sharing this food of our thoughts.

In this sacred space we can remember that the door post of the wigwam is an important place where the Sacred Worlds of our ancestors come into balance. If we are strong enough, we can take a journey. We can let the sound of the sacred drum guide and protect us on this journey.

Much of my work in spiritual counselling takes me to other worlds where people sometimes get stuck, or where they might need to go, whether they are aware of this or not. Mostly people today are not aware. Mostly in today's world, people are pretty dull from all the noise, pollution, busy lifestyle, and distraction.

I have always been different. Since my youth I sought the lonely path. Great Spirit was over my life. That caused me a lot of confusion. But I learned to live with it, there wasn't much choice. For many years I decided to close up shop. I said to Spirit, leave me alone. I don't want any new insights and most importantly, I don't want to know any more about other people's burdens or worries!

But my life wasn't that simple. By closing the door to Spirit, I made myself sick physically and in every other way. A healer cannot always choose to turn off the energy. Energy flows. Healing is found in one way or another. That is just how it has been in my life, strange as it seems.

The sound of the drum sometimes disturbs your awareness. Then you go off in a new direction. Once the doorpost of the Wigwam called me down into the underworld... In that place I met new people that I never knew existed. They were a lot like people up here, but they also had different perspectives. Some were deeply depressed. Some were really creative, and they could make beautiful quill work boxes and weave with strands of wood. While others formed manipulative plans that were quite detailed and involved. They often appeared busy with their work but more buzzing in their minds.

Sometimes people exist within us that we never knew before. Sometimes they are parts of other people we come across and we may wish we never went that way. But life is like this. For some folks who are on the healing or teaching path in life — we cannot always choose to isolate ourselves from new experiences!

Other times people quietly ask me, without saying a word, to journey to the world above the earth. They are often seeking something they never experienced before. But they don't know that yet. How can we seek something we do not know exists?

I've met many folks who go the round of many psychologists and counsellors, and later on they end up with me. The sad but true state of affairs is that most therapists today have little imagination. After nearly two decades of teaching therapists, I can say that we teach new counsellors too much theory and not enough real life. From little things, big things grow.

So, in the world above the earth I have met some really wonderful but strange people too. Funny thing is... they mostly look the same as people down here. But they think in different ways. Or maybe it is me who thinks in new ways in new worlds. Some of these folks up there are pretty deeply in tune. They might just want you to sit in their wigwam for a while and share a meal. Sometimes this is good, and fellowship is wonderful. I've returned to the seeking person with fresh insight on their issues we both never expected. Other times when sharing a meal in the world up there, you might watch your back.

One thing seems true. You don't tend to stay long in different worlds. Most of my trips are for a purpose, and with a fair bit of preparation and follow-up once I get back. Rituals of respect are important. Giving back is always a must. Up there are many ways forward it seems to me. Down there are many insights from deep wells. Regardless, we might find something we are looking for. Or we might just see a part of ourselves that is quite funny.

What is most amazing is when spirits from other worlds come to visit us around the Fire in our Wigwam. Should be no surprise. We open a Sacred Circle here too. This was how I met Greywolf for the first time. We danced around the fire light together and fell down biting each other in playfulness. The stars are all around us when we least expect it. Even during overcast skies.

So then, all of life is still Sacred. Regardless what the others might want us to believe.

The best of modern science and psychotherapy suggests that the ancient and balanced Teachings of our Elders are true and ought to be respected as such. My journey into other worlds, including the modern material worlds around the earth today, tells me that coming home to our traditions is a good thing. How we reclaim our heritage and come to terms with the deep spiritual meaning is a wonderful journey. In this way, the Sacred Worlds of our Ancestors are coming back into balance. This is our pathwork for today and for tomorrow. This is our autumn preparation for the winter to come

Reflection

During the New Moon of this month, consider your own personal story and write about your path in life. What were your major realisations that helped you along the way? What spiritual experiences led you to be curious about what this book contained? What led you to buy or find this book? What do you hope to gain from reading?

Recording these insights may help you touch base with some of your inner purpose. What we seek is often related to what we hope to become. What we seek is also a lot to do with what we wish to find. The two may seem the same at first sight, but rarely are they in fact the same.

What you seek is what seems obvious to you now. What you wish to find is something quite different, and may be more in tune with your dreams, hopes and fears about life. Our wishes are often much more creative and expansive than what we seek today. And both things are important.

The reflection during this moon time was about Sacred Worlds we live in and visit over time. What Sacred Worlds do you live in? This may surprise you, but how you describe your world will be very different from how anyone else will describe that same world. In fact, no two worlds are alike in all ways. Human beings are spiritual beings. As such we all have unique perspectives. We can share consensual reality with each other - so our worlds can overlap. A sign of a healthy society is when people share a certain degree of consensual reality, and a certain degree of personal and creative realities. A society built on solid ground allows people the freedom to define their own world views.

Your worldview is unique to you. In this book you are sharing a tiny bit of my worldview, although I must say that my views change and evolve rather quickly. As I am reviewing these readings, I am reminded that they were written several years ago already, and my views have already changed in significant ways. This is all OK.

In editing this book of reflections, it seems important to respect the way things were written by that person who wrote them during the past. His views were important at that time. We can respect that and learn much from his teachings.

He wrote these reflections for a regional monthly periodical with a specific intention to speak to the Mi'kmaq people from his particular range of perspectives. He was on the Medicine Path. He was already a psychotherapist. He had many years of experience in the western academe. He was already a seasoned author and researcher, clinical supervisor and leader in his fields of practice. He wanted to give back to his people.

As I am reading these reflections several years later, I am moved by his insights. Even though they were written for a specific purpose, they seem to ring true in a different time and place. The readings feel timeless and able to speak to people in many different places.

You too will learn so much. This is what life is all about. Your story will also change over time. But certain things will ring true over the years. This is how you will find your identity, your sense of purpose. Sometimes identity is about what stays true over many years, and in a strange way identity is also about what changes the most. When you get a sense of these things, you will know more about who you are. M'sit No'koma. Ta'ho.

Sacred Teachings

Toqa'q/Autumn Moons

October Wikewiku's Animal-fattening Moon

Pjila'si ~ Welcome, come in, sit down.

Last month we explored working in sacred space. This article looks at listening to our dreams. What do we mean by dreams? Well, several years ago I would tell you that dreams happen when we sleep. I would then tell you that dreams are a physiological function of the human mind and body, and what we call the unconscious. Then I might have talked about Freud who suggested that the dreams we remember telling us about what we are missing in our life today. Jung his disciple disagreed with Freud and said that dreams are doorways to the collective human unconscious, a spiritual realm we all share.

But today my feelings for dreams are much expanded by living in Australia with Aboriginal people. What I have learned is from friends who share their stories with me. Aboriginal Australians share what is called the Dreamtime. The Creator Spirit is often called the Dreamtime Serpent. This Serpent is known by most if not all of the tribes across the Great Land. This Being wove her or his way throughout the country. As the Being passed into new tribal countries different Dreaming Law was created and given to the Old People. That Dreaming was placed in each Tribal Country. Language, Ceremony, Song Lines, Dancing and Culture all grew from these Original Teachings. These Laws were handed down through countless generations. This is an Ancient Land.

There is old tribal memory, I have been told, of a time long ago when all the lands on earth were one big landmass. Here I have heard this called Gondwana Land. Some friends suggest the white fellah myth of human origins from Africa is absurd, and the myth of only 40,000 years of migration into Australia by Aboriginal people is also crazy and too convenient for the colonisers. Indeed. Sound familiar?

Dreams must be more than we are told in the mainstream myths. Being challenged in Australia by powerful teachings encouraged me to learn about our Old Teachings. This led me to discover the Mi'kmaw Sacred Worlds. This worldview, or cosmology, is a powerful teaching for today. Just as powerful as it was for the Old Ones of the People. Reflecting on what Australians call the Dreaming, in my feeling for Mi'kmaw ways the word 'Medicine' seems similar. In these insights, we know we can never know exactly how things once were. But our Spirits know what feels right and we listen to the Elders for guidance and for correction too.

Through the Dreaming and the Medicine, we vision and journey. The sound of the Drum carries us across the worlds. The Drumbeat carries us to the Heart of Creation. In Australia the Clap Stick and Didgeridoo carry the Dancer through the Dreaming Song Lines. Across these traditions the healer or seer transforms their awareness. They move out of their body and their regular way of knowing. They shift into new realms as their work demands. The work of healing and gaining insight demands much from the practitioner. This kind of cultural Ritual or Ceremony challenges many current ideas. Today's material world no longer has the skills or depth to understand or to respect. Even in counselling, health, and medicine people are lost unless they can see simple explanation, poke a needle in it, or draw blood. Modern ways are quite hollow, shallow, and cold compared to cultural forms of healing, change, and transformation.

You might ask, why am I interested in these experiences? The first answer is rational. Subtle forms of awareness arising in Culture and Ceremony reveal our human capacity for intuition, insight, emotional and social growth, and the healing of our identity. These pathways give us enormous inner and social resources. These are largely lost to modern science. Although, I do know many scientists who are open minded and who gain much from these methods of inquiry and the perspectives that come from the Dreaming and Medicine Traditions.

The second answer is also rational but lies in my dreams. Since childhood dreams have guided me, pushed and prodded me. Visions invaded my youth in big ways and changed my life and behaviour. Spiritual experiences shocked me in many ways, having never been prepared or properly trained. Most of us are unprepared for what life throws at us. We also live in very spiritual times, when the earth and people are awakening in new ways.

This reminds me of the story of the Wise Owl. He was an Old One and liked to watch the forest from the higher branches while the young ones learned to hunt. One of the young ones was very curious. She wanted to find out what it looked like above the highest branches. She asked the Old One. He said, 'Maybe one day soon.' She was content for many moons with this answer. Then one day she was talking with a friend, 'Isn't it long enough now? My wings are strong. I can do it; I know I can.' Her friend got it in his head to go and look, just take a peek, and let her know if it was safe. One day while all the other young ones were busy, he flew off quietly into the bush. Rising higher and higher, he thought no one was watching. The Old One was aware, and before he got too far, the Old One sang out – 'Heads up to all the young ones! Time for a teaching tale! Gather in the circle!' The young one flying off heard the song, and realised he better show up, so he turned around quick like and made for the circle.

In the circle all the young ones gathered to hear their Elder tell the stories of their people. Some were excited, others bored, but all had respect in their hearts. The Old One started his tale, 'Once during the Old Days, when the Old Ones of the People were strong, brave, free and could fly anywhere they chose, two little ones got it in their heads to take off into the blue sky above the highest branches.' The young ones looked each other in the eye. They said nothing. But they were asking each other, how does he know that?

The Old One continued, 'Those two young ones were very brave and strong.' The two little owls smiled at each other with pride. 'They knew their wings had grown a lot over the past few moons. They got it in their heads to take a look above the branches.' All the little owls let out a gasp of air and some said, 'no, really?' The Wise Owl then said, 'The word spread to the other young ones. Some felt, no way, we won't do that, we won't go that high up! Others said, our place is right here. We are staying home! Still others argued, why not, we are bored here! And a particular young one went off alone, and quietly thought it all through for a very long time...' The Old Owl turned his face as if to think...

Then the Old Owl said, 'After much consideration that young one decided to pray.' All the little owls looked at each other as if to say, 'Gosh, that must be serious business.' 'Yes, that young one asked Creator for some insight.' They all let out another gasp of air. Imagine talking directly to the Creator! They were very surprised. Many had never heard they could even try to do that kind of Ceremony. The Elder then said, 'That young one had a good heart. She didn't want for herself alone. She sought a vision for Our People. That was why she prayed with such courage.'

The Wise Owl looked around and chewed on his Tobacco. He looked up to the sky for a long time, as if remembering something he forgot to say. The little ones in the circle sat as quiet as a pin. You couldn't even hear their breathing. As if speaking from very far away, the Old One whispered, 'One day... Later on, down the track... That young one who sought a vision came into the Circle, where everyone was gathered for a feast. She gathered up her Courage. She asked the Elder of the People to say a word. Then everyone listened... She said, 'I heard about the World Above the Earth. Where the highest branches cannot even begin to reach. I Waited and Prayed. Long time I waited. Long time I cried for a Vision. Then it came to me.' She fell silent. Her head fell down.

Everyone stopped, listened, looked. She cried many tears. But her heart swelled with Pride and with Power. Her wings began to shiver. It was like the Spirit of Creator was over her body. The Elder stepped close. Reached out his powerful wings to cover her. Everyone waited with respect. They knew a Sacred Time was Upon Them. When he was ready, he said to the People, 'Let this young one's Vision inspire, challenge, and teach. She sees her path well. There is courage in facing the Unknown Worlds beyond our own. There is courage in Staying with the Familiar. Each path is important for our tribe. Each way will be honoured.'

Mainstream theory does not understand these things very well. They misunderstand Aboriginal people who are often closer to intuitive insight and spiritual connections. Instead of seeing this as strength, it is often viewed with fear or misunderstanding. Often labels of mental health are used where they are not appropriate, and where a wholistic approach to helping would make life easier for people who are suffering. By coming to terms with Indigenous traditions many things in life make more sense. But no one else is going to take this challenge in our place. Each one of us must choose. What do we rely on when we say 'Aboriginal'? Where is our heart and focus?

In today's world it is possible to awaken from sleep and listen to our dreams, and to reconnect with the spiritual technologies of the past. Traditions are alive and well. I believe this very much. As a therapist I am constantly amazed by how creative and powerful people really are. Our Ancestors are alive within us, asking us to choose to love with truth and integrity. If we are open enough to listen, we can hear them singing to us. If we have enough courage, we will begin to sing back to them. Then a new Circle will open up, and new balance may return to the world.

Reflection

Place yourself in the Wise Old Owl story. What character are you? Why do you identify with one of the characters?

Sacred Teachings

Explore the meaning of this for yourself. Give it time. If you feel so inclined, write another story based on your character's worldview. Remember our last moon time when we celebrated and acknowledged your unique worldview. Well, here is your chance. Write a short story or just dream up a story that reflects the worldview you share with your character. When you are ready, share your story with a friend, or with your children. They too might like to join in and create their own version of the story, or a new story all together. Send your stories to Earth Rattle Publishing so that a book of short stories might arise from these well springs of inspiration and wisdom. M'sit No'koma. Ta'ho.

Joseph Randolph Bowers

November Keptekewiku's River-freezing Moon

Pjila'si ~ Welcome, come in, sit down.

Last month we explored listening to our dreams. This article will explore issues of faith from the Eagle's eye. To explain where I am coming from, some history might help. I grew up in the Roman Catholic faith. When a youngster, my sister found the evangelical church. Through her, I experienced a 'born again' moment. My parents in their worry opened themselves to the renewal movement sweeping the Catholic world. They got me back to the fold, and in my youth, I enjoyed a few years of music ministry and work in various parishes.

Later on, I completed a Bachelor in Religious Studies. The program was run by professors who were x-priests, and they were fairly liberal in their views. This gave me critical sociology, an approach that questions assumptions and asks many difficult questions. The status of women was a big issue then. I remember the first time my professor told us we can no longer use the word 'man' to mean both men and women. Times were changing...

Through the critical analysis of faith, my childhood faith fell apart. Many people thought I would become a priest. But my learning highlighted the contradictions in the church. This turned me toward a secular career. The contradictions included the abuse of children by priests and brothers; gay and lesbian rights; and women's lack of place in the leadership of the church. After much thought and prayer, I decided to protest the injustices of Catholicism by fasting from the sacraments. This was a time when I saw the Priesthood and the Mass as being used as instruments of oppression by a Church that had lost its way. What began as a temporary decision to fast from the Eucharist lasted for over fifteen years. You might think, so what? But if you have any idea of what this means to a very devote and mystical-oriented Catholic, you will begin to realise the extent of this decision.

During that time further study led to a Master's degree in Education and Counselling. I was honoured to study under the late Redge Craig who many will remember as a pioneer in the marriage renewal movement, and as a champion of Aboriginal rights. He received the Eagle Feather in honour of his work. He also trained social workers in the Maritime region of Canada for over two decades as a professor at the School of Social Work. Redge's advice led me to deepen my commitment to protest and to finding a new way for myself that was apart from the church.

Along a winding road, somehow, I ended up with a PhD teaching and research scholarship in Australia. Another story for another day... The PhD focused on minority issues for gay and lesbian people. From that I learned that homophobia, negative attitudes toward gay people, are a big problem in the fields of counselling, health, and education. Like with racism, there is much work to do in improving conditions for minority people. Racism and homophobia are forms of prejudice, and prejudice is a big issue as any minority person can tell you.

After the PhD, life asked me to revisit issues of faith. I believe the Eagle had Her eye on me. She had a different vision for my life. It was then that I sadly realised the Roman church had not moved forward on any of these social justice issues. Indeed, many people suggested the church had become more fundamentalist and narrower in views. As I researched the issues again, I became aware of other abuses in Latin America, and of the mistreatment of Aboriginal people around the world under the rules of orthodoxy. For example, the same problems with the abuse of children were rampant in Australia. Roman politics were to simply close down churches in western countries while building churches in third world countries where people are generally less educated and have less choices, all the while not changing their practices. These realisations deepened my resolve to find another way. Visits to remote Aboriginal communities devastated by the church profoundly moved me – there must be a way toward healing.

Then something surprised me. I found an independent catholic movement of churches that exists apart from Rome, with groups in Australia, America, the UK, Canada, and in other countries. At the time I contacted a Bishop in this movement and after much discussion and preparation, he ordained me a priest in the apostolic tradition. The ordination was a profound moment for me. In that ceremony I felt the connection back through history to Jesus. In that experience I knew Jesus to be a tribal man, an Indigenous man, and a Chief and Medicine Man.

The people around me affirmed this in different ways, as Aboriginal Australian friends celebrated this Ceremony with me, and I wore priestly garments decorated by Australian Aboriginal Dreamtime images.

My dream of fulfilling issues of faith from an Eagle's eye was now grounded in an Indigenous vision for church and for building community in the spirit of our traditions. Eagle's vision tells me that the Indian Red Road of spirituality existed eons before Christianity. But in any case, for me the ability to pray the Mass is a great gift. This is just part of my upbringing. The ritual opens me up to goodness, mystical connection, and healing energy. I can see no reason why this ritual should be restricted to Roman priests. 'Catholic' does mean universal, after all. Indeed, in many parts of the world the Mass is not restricted as we have been told. In these ways my Mi'kmaw and French Acadian heritage naturally honours a catholic orientation to life. This is still a part of me and is brought into the contemporary world in new ways that are based in an Aboriginal spirituality.

The next step was to acknowledge that the Roman language of the Mass is foreign to me, and to let it go from my prayer. Great Spirit moved my heart to re-write the ritual into the 'Mass of Creation' using words and images that honour the Aboriginal way. This form of prayer gives peace of heart. It brings together in harmony the two spiritual traditions that mean most to me. This form of prayer is based in an Aboriginal philosophy and theology. One day I may sit with these experiences and write a book based on the Mi'kmaw Mass of Creation.

Coming from a wholistic perspective, faith and spirituality are central to health and wellbeing. For each person, if we take up our path in life and follow our vision with any seriousness, we will have to ask some basic questions. These questions lead us to new meaning. Meaning leads us to make choices about what we believe. What we believe takes us on a new journey that echoes the challenges and stories of Great Whale, Eagle, Wolf, and many of our Ancestors whose spirits and journeys brought us into being.

If spirituality is how we make our meaning in life, then faith is how we live that meaning. For me, Aboriginal spirituality is a living faith that challenges the status quo in mainstream Canadian, Australian, and American contexts. Not to mention dozens of other countries around the world. Indigenous people champion the rights of Mother Earth through our deep faith and spiritual traditions. Be challenged, inspired, and proud in your Aboriginal heart. Remember the sound of the drum. This is an important part of the story of how I came to see issues of faith from the Eagle's eye. Our Stories are our Medicine.

Reflection

During this New Moon, consider again your own story. What challenges were you given in your life to resolve, unravel, or explore? What unresolved issues were you given by your parents or grandparents? In the story shared above the seeker had many challenges. He grew up in a world where certain beliefs were dominant. As he got older, he needed to make his own decisions about what he would believe and why. In his case, he decided to keep certain parts of his upbringing and to change other aspects. In so doing, he moved away from certain views that were shared with people in his past.

We are all like this in our own ways. We grow up with beliefs given to us by our parents and the world around us. We have to choose as we get older what we will believe and why. We often keep some of what we were given and change other bits and pieces as we go along. We might change a whole heap, and then later reconnect with some bits from our past that feel important or worth revisiting. Life is like this. What is your story of growing up, changing and evolving? M'sit No'koma. Ta'ho.

December Kjiku's The great moon

Pjila'si ~ Welcome, come in, sit down.

Last month we explored faith from the Eagle's eye. This article will share stories of my time in Australia. Living in Australia has been a wonderful experience that taught me much about who I am, and about Indigenous issues. Coming this far away from home started with seeking a vision.

My heart turned to prayer while working in counselling practice in rural Nova Scotia. Something inside me looked around the world for an opportunity to learn, grow, and take up the healing path as the focus of my life. That door opened when offered a PhD teaching and research scholarship.

When I arrived in Sydney, Australia for the first time the trip was completely on faith that things would work out. When I arrived at my host's home no one was there. In a tired jet legged state, the first thing I saw was a lemon tree. Growing up in the cold north of Canada, I had never seen a lemon tree. The sight of lemons ripe for picking on the tree was like a vision in a dream. I just stood there and started to weep.

My host's neighbour looked out from her window and saw me crying. That was pretty funny. The look on her face was precious! It made me smile. She came out, took my arm and led me to the front door. She had a key. My host had told her that I was coming and to let me in. She took me into the flat and showed me around. Then I was left alone. It was all so surreal. If you have ever travelled 18,000 miles in one stretch without much breaks and only pit stops in a busy airport, you will know immediately what I mean by surreal. Your body is tired and worn out, and your perception of things becomes very dreamlike.

The first thing to do was to sit on the floor and pray. I did not have any Sage or other herb except what I carried in my Medicine Pouch around my neck. People travelling to Australia are not allowed to take in organic material like plants. The only herb that I had was hiding in the Medicine Pouch that I had shown to the Customs Officer. They let me through with what I had. I was very grateful.

At that time, I took a bit of the tiny amount that was there and burned it in thanks and in respect for the Ancestors of this land of Australia. Later on, when I got inland to my destination, my instinct led me to seek out an Elder and ask permission to come into the local tribal country. Having never learned proper protocol in the past, these instincts were always a surprise and a big learning for me.

My early days here were amazing. My senses were always alert, everything was different, the climate, sun, air, earth, and people were all so different. My spirit was so alive. Dreams and visions came to me. Powerful healing came for certain people in need. Life is not always like this. It was very unusual. A real high. Then the valley hit.

Through many encounters I learned about Aboriginal Australia, and eventually met a beautiful Aboriginal soul mate who shared life with me for over ten years. These years brought new opportunities. I was asked to teach and coordinate a Diploma in Aboriginal Family and Community Counselling. This program introduced me to many people from all across Australia.

Requests then came to visit communities. At one stage I went all the way to Broome in North Western Australia. That is a trip like from Halifax to Vancouver, then up to Alaska. A fair stretch. Up there I worked with counsellors and helpers whose work included addressing the trauma created by the stolen generations of people forcibly removed from their families and communities. We visited a few remote Aboriginal communities, and learned about the challenges, issues and joys that people felt in those places. We shared local stories and learned the Rainbow Serpent Dance. That was a great honour. All the rest of that day we could see the Serpent in the form of clouds in the sky. It was so clear and seen by all of us, it was truly amazing. What struck me about our time together was how similar the stories are of loss, grief, violence, and disrespect shown by the invader and coloniser to Aboriginal people whether in Canada or in Australia. This made me realise many things.

The more I studied colonial history from an Indigenous point of view, the more the truth hits home. Many of our sorrows and sufferings are not about us. The history and how it played out, and how that manifests today, was not of our choosing.

When friends in Australia tell me about their great grandparents, aunties and uncles, who were rounded up like cattle and shot dead; it just sends shivers up your spine. It reminds me of stories about Nazi Germany and the gas chambers. In Australia, instead of gas chambers, water holes were poisoned. In a desert country, the tribe and the native animals depend totally on the water holes. The invader knew this and saw fit to destroy the source of life from the People. A People who Creator placed in this country as the rightful Custodian.

In visiting some of the locations where these mass murders occurred, people with sensitive spirits can feel the memory and energy of these happenings. The location Remembers. There are no monuments. Third and fourth generation European descendants still want to deny and forget. But the Land will not forget this violence to the First People. These Living Memories of the violence and horrors of invasion are pretty close to people in Australia. The history here is only about two hundred years. Then there are the stolen generation memories here that are very much present, much like the residential school memories in Canada.

Where I live in New South Wales, on the East Coast of Australia, the issues people face is pretty similar to home in some ways. The divide and conquer tactics of government are everywhere to be seen here. Instead of reserves we have missions, many of which were church based places of great historical suffering. Many Aboriginal people live in homes throughout towns and cities, a form of 'integration' policies that serve to further isolate families from each other. This makes it even harder if not impossible for communities and Nations to form cohesive identities and policies. For this reason, local clans are mostly divided with little or no leadership. This leads me to conclude that while some people say the reserves in Canada are a crime and places of poverty, etc... After seeing tribes completely separated and living in mainstream houses across a city, without a central community, and with little or no social cohesion that draws people together as one Nation, I tend to think that reserves and missions are not as bad after all.

Forced upon our own personal, individual survival, we are made very weak and powerless in the face of the massive mainstream machine of economics, political and social norms, and the customs of the nation state that dominates Aboriginal people's lives. Then the rhetoric of health care and education come to play. Then the negative images of Aboriginal people in the press that are promoted by governments to keep the majority content in their ignorance are other tactics we observe.

Seeing these things in another country makes it even more clear for me that the issues we face are not really about us. These tactics of prejudice, violence, and the many enduring efforts toward the genocide of Aboriginal people are simply about power and control of the land, natural resources, and the stubborn refusal to acknowledge and uphold Aboriginal Sovereignty and Self Government. The government in Australia, much like Canada, has become a symbol of the entrenched racist attitudes that lie under the surface of the country's policies and shadowy heritage. Here too people look to the political leader to say sorry, and to mean it in reality. But sadly, that custom of integrity seems foreign to the European and British tradition of law and governance.

Where these issues play with wholistic health and Traditional Medicine is all too clear. The pressures of our marginal place in society increase our family's burdens. We must seek our cultural strengths to help us to cope. As a minority, we might find ourselves playing out our anxiety by harming ourselves, our families, and our communities. When we stand divided, our house will fall. This principle is true in each person, in families, and in communities. And it is true for the Mi'kmaq Nation and for other First Nations.

Our health and wellbeing are intimately tied up with our political and social struggles for empowerment. The economics and the natural dynamics of our daily lives are central to the picture. How we choose to work with our circumstances is up to us. To move forward there is much work to be done by everyone. What a great work we are into now. Our own re-creation. To do this with hope, courage, and strength of character is a great personal and collective goal. We can share that goal more and more. Stand strong Mi'kmaq First Nation. Stand in oneness, like your Creator. Prayers are sung for you from this great land of Australia, where roses bloom in winter and where your night is but another day of dreams and good visions. While you sleep, my prayers are with you through the day.

Reflection

This Moon time is not considered the 'new cycle' or new year in Aboriginal cosmology. But because the mainstream idea of new year is so deeply embedded in our psyche, it may be useful to celebrate this Moon tide as an opportunity to reflect upon the year past.

Incidentally, the new cycle moon in the Mi'kmaw cosmology, in my understanding, is April Penatemuiku's Egg Laying Moon. There are many who say it is actually this moon, Kjiku's The Great Moon, because the shortest day of the year happens during this cycle. This parallels the darkness of the New Moon and so ties the whole year together. From the shortest day arises the growth of the moons toward the peak of summertime.

These two temporal and light-bearing poles represent the turning of the tides of the year.

Likewise, there are others who say that the Spring Moon holds the same kind of spiritual, temporal and ecological potential and power. It is balanced by the Sacred Moon of Autumn, and both are changing seasons such that their power is greater. Therefore, the new year happens during springtime. That same year begins passing away during autumn. Funny enough, some say the year begins with Autumn, because this is when the Seed Falls from the Tree and dies, hides in the soil, and is reborn in Spring. These are all amazing and rich Traditions that show the diversity of opinion, and the many insights that lead us to deeper respect of our environment. Personally, I find all of these Traditions hold a wealth of wisdom and insight. This leaves me many new year days to celebrate! In the course of my life, the more celebrations the better!

I therefore invite you to consider your journey so far. Take a review of your journal entries, your artwork, or your paintings, your crochet work, or your collecting of natural bits and pieces from your environment. Remember now to sit with these Blessings. Remember any gifts given to you. Insights. Little moments of pleasure. Times of peace or rest. Moments of celebrating during your Full Moons. Remember any gifts that others gave to you this year. Gifts of time. Consideration. Patience. Kindness. Give thanks for these gifts and experiences by offering a pinch of Sacred Tobacco to Mother Earth. You can place this under a tree or somewhere people will not walk.

You can also make a Mi'kmaw Prayer Tie by using some red cotton cloth. Cut the cloth in a triangle. Place your pile of Tobacco in your left palm. Cover with your right hand. Feel the energy of your Prayer moving from your heart into the Tobacco. Place your intentions into the mix. Ask Creator for a special blessing for your loved ones. When you are finished, take the

Tobacco and place it in the middle of the red triangle. Tie all three ends by making as many knots as you need to secure the bundle into place. Then find some string or small twine and wrap around the Prayer Tie where the knots are tied. Leave about one foot or three hundred millimetres of string free. You can then take the Prayer Tie to one of your favourite trees. Ask permission from the Tree. If you feel all is OK, go ahead and tie the Prayer Tie up in the tree. The Prayer Tie can dangle from one of the branches. As you do this, give thanks and ask the Spirit of the Tree for protection and guidance in fulfilling the wishes of your prayer. You, the Sacred Tree, its branches, and the Sun, Moon and Stars are all witness to your prayerful intention.

M'sit No'koma. Ta'ho.

Sacred Teachings

The Second Moon Cycle: Year Two

Joseph Randolph Bowers

Kesik/Winter Moons

January Punamujuiku's Frost Fish Moon

Pjila'si ~ Welcome, come in, sit down.

During Punamujuiku's Frost Fish Moon we acknowledge the Powers of the North, Sacred Turtle Medicine and the Old Grandmothers of the Mi'kmaq Nation. We remember the Welcome Pipe of our families that were once kept by so many. We remember the culturally integrated ceremonies that brought us together in respect, honour, humility, and justice.

During the Frost Fish Moon a tiny bit of wisdom comes to those of us who pray in the old ways. Do you remember how we preserve foods to last through the winter? Remember that we preserve meat, fish, berry, tea – all kinds of preserves that locked in the goodness and nutritional value of our natural foods? We instinctively know how important preserving food is for our survival. We also know it takes a lot of work, and preparation.

The life-skills involved in food preservation include many skills that we need to revive today in our modern communities. These include thinking through steps involved, following through with a commitment, learning from mistakes along the way, improving as you go, and resting after hours of hard work. Practical skills include knowing how to gather different foods, knowing how much to gather and not taking too much, gauging the environment for the best time to gather, knowing how to care for the foods that are gathered, and knowing how to preserve different foods in various ways.

Food storage is also a very important skill, because foods can easily be lost. Foods need to be protected through the long months of winter until it is time for them to be eaten with thanksgiving and prayer.

This reminds me of similar lessons about how to carry Sacred Medicines. Someone new to the old ways may receive Sacred Medicine and not be aware of how to care for the Medicine. Basic skills need to be learned. For example, Sacred Feathers can be kept in a birch bark 'Wigwam' or Container, lined with a worked Deer hide or soft fabric. People today also use hard cardboard covered with fabric, kept together like a long book that opens on one side, and tied with ribbons.

Sacred Feathers like all other Medicines ask us to preserve their power and integrity. We learn these skills by treating the Medicines with great respect. We give each Medicine a special home or wigwam. When coming out of their wigwam we smudge with sacred herb like sage or sweet grass. We cleanse our bodies, hearts, and minds before holding precious gifts of Creator.

This reminds me of how we once felt about all the foods that we ate. Even today the good foods we eat are Sacred Medicines for our health. Food comes to us with great cost to the animal and plant spirits who give their life so we may live. Sacred Medicines teach us about valuing food. Valuing food can teach us about caring for Medicines.

Reflection

During this New Moon of the mainstream's new year, take some time to reflect on your basic needs in life. Needs are different from wants and desires. Your needs are like food, water, shelter, family, love and safety. Needs form the basic boundaries of respect for yourself, your loved ones, and your society. When people step outside of basic needs, they enter into the land of wants and desires, and this is when things tend to get a little messier. We can easily lose respect for what is basic to life.

Food is a good example. People need a basic amount of food to survive. When working to an optimum, the human body tends to be lean and mean. But when people go beyond what they need, and start wanting and desiring more and more yummy foods, they are working in a different level. That brings its own rewards and outcomes, many of which are not all that good to our health and length of life.

Traditional attitudes and beliefs about food are based on the natural scarcity of resources. We give thanks to Creator for our meal, because we know that our life depends on the natural world, the creatures who sacrifice their Life for us, and the Spirits of the Plants who offer themselves to our wellbeing.

Consider your diet and food intake. Make a list of the foods you eat. How much is healthy foods? How much is fatty foods? How much is meat-based foods? How much is veggies and salads and what percentage is organic?

How healthy are you physically? What needs to change for your health to improve? What spiritual issues come up for you when you reflect on these questions? How can you bring your diet back to a more balanced and Traditional diet, without all the modern-day unhealthy fats and sugars? Take some serious time to ask yourself about your health. And make some basic plans. What changes will you make to your diet? To your exercise? To your foods chosen. To your eating out and fast food habits? To your eating of veggies, fruit and other healthy things?

Make the link to your spiritual practice clear. Why are you changing your lifestyle, in what ways, and what will this bring for you in future? See your intention clearly. Make a Sacred Prayer Tie and put all of these intentions into the Sacred Tobacco. Hang the Prayer Tie in a Special Place that you can see every day, to remind you of the commitment and choices you are making for the sake of your spiritual and physical well-being. M'sit No'koma. Ta'ho.

Joseph Randolph Bowers

February Apiknajit Snow Blinder Moon

Pjila'si ~ Welcome, come in, sit down.

Come in out of the cold! Share the warmth of this Sacred Fire during Apiknajit, Snow Blinder Moon. During this moon we acknowledge the Powers of the North are very present to us. Our Ancestors very near. We call into our hearts the Powers of the South to bring warmth when we most need strength. We honour Paq'tism, Wolf whose eyes bring the warm energy of the sun into the deepest, darkest forest.

It is no surprise that during the height of winter moons the depths of our heart arises and breaks into our dreams and waking moments. We can come close to the sacred this time of year. This is the time of year when many of our Elders pass over into the Spirit World. This is when our own spirits need healing. This is when many a memory of trauma comes into our mind asking for strength to transform into a Caterpillar.

In spite of the hectic modern world, if we are wise, we bring ourselves to the Sacred Fire. The Fire honours, teaches, and inspires every person regardless. There is no better teacher. Fire warms, smoke cleanses. Embers tell stories of days not so long past. Many a Sacred Fire gives sparks that pull light into our future.

During Apiknajit Snow Blinder Moon the future becomes today as the past is transformed into the present moment. This is a special time of year to enter the Seventh Sacred Direction. The seventh Direction is the way of spiritual growth, personal awareness.

When Muin, Bear sleeps human spirits also enter a spiritual calm. But only when we are prepared to give ourselves time to rest. This means our prior summer and autumn were filled with practical work in the world so that during this Moon we can have time to sit by the Sacred Fire.

Even when we forget these ways, life pushes our bodies to remember. We create crisis in spite of ourselves. Spirit breaks into our lives.

The Old Laws of our People are not far away. In fact, the wisdom of our environment comes to light when our awareness shifts.

It is that simple. That close to us. That real.

Ask that part of you that asks for help, 'Please be a seed within me that becomes a Caterpillar. During this Moon of Deep Snows, I will carry you and protect you.' Treat your inner self with tenderness and love. You too are a Sacred Medicine.

Do not expect your hurting part to transform into a Butterfly, not right away. Give that time. No one really knows when the Caterpillar becomes a Butterfly. But we do know that Butterflies cannot be rushed. Their wings will gain strength during the moons ahead.

During the Spring Moons then, you may not even realise when one day you can fly! Healing is so natural, so gentle. It just takes time.

Reflection

What does it mean that our Ancestors are very near to us? What does it really mean that the Sacred Fire in this Wigwam offers safety, comfort and solace from the wider world?

On one hand our Ancestor's presence gives us rest, because we are at home with them, they are our kin. This brings renewal to our spirit. We can retreat from the conflicts of the world around us, and from the energies of the wider world, into this Sacred Place we call home, family, and heart. This is a form of quiet time. We can genuinely feel from the heart and offer our being to the Sacred Fire. This may be done by only giving our time - we sit by the Fire with our Elders near and far. We may offer a pinch of Sacred Tobacco, made Sacred by Mother Earth, and by our offering in a feeling of giving, caring, loving. We can then centre our minds within our heart. This is called finding peace.

And all of these Ways could be called prayer, but the word prayer might feel like a nasty word because of its religious meanings. We might feel like "prayer" is taboo. We may also feel that "ceremony" or "ritual" are also taboo. These are things that other people do when they are engaging in "religious" activities. Many people today do not want to go there. That is OK. We are all "in recovery" from a very difficult past where religion was used to dominate, abuse and control people, especially Indigenous people. We need to find a path through those feelings of taboo, where we can still recover the Truth, Power and Beauty of our heritage. And this is true of all people in western societies, as we are all on a journey of recovery in one form or other.

On the other hand, our Ancestors being close to us means that we are called to live in Truth, Power and Beauty. This means that our path in life needs to embody Listening, Humility, Justice and Compassion. These four pillars of the Wigwam are so Powerful because they are Spiritual Foundations upon which human life, relationships and family are built and sustained. Our Ancestors who have moved into the Spirit World are in touch with the Higher Powers of Love, Faith, Hope and Truth. In the World of Spirit, they are Dancing the Original Dance, the Dreaming Dance, the First Medicine Dance. We have their help, love and patience but we also have their hope, fire and sense of right and wrong.

Coming back to our Old Ways means we are finding a sure path into the future. We are searching for the foundations to living that will help us survive, thrive and prosper. We are looking for basic values that will help us know right from wrong. We are needing to have strong boundaries because the world around us, and the wider world, have their own agenda and want us to spin out of control - to become robot consumers with little to no values, so that it is easy to manipulate people and the environment to suit our wants and desires. People in the modern world forget what they actually need and are focused on wants and desires above all else.

These forms of unbalanced beliefs and lifestyle make our generations some of the most selfish that have ever lived on this planet. Sorry, but what do you think our Ancestors are saying? What do you feel from their hearts as you see them standing around our Sacred Fire? They are feeling we have lost our way.

They are often weeping for what we have lost, let go of so easily, and given away without regard or respect.

Reflect during this Sacred Ancient Moon that your Ancestors want to support you, but they also want you to wake up. They want you to see clearly. This Sacred Fire not only provides warmth, comfort and safety. Because this Fire is Sacred, the Spirit of Flames exists in Sacred Relationship to You, Your Spirit and Life. The Spirit Fire asks you to Awaken. Your Spirit is asked to Dance. This means you are invited and even drawn into the Original Dance of Creation whether you want to be or not - you are here, after all. You have decided to witness this Truth. You are Ready and Willing to Awaken.

The Arms of Spirit Fire call you, beckon you, and embrace you to take on a life of Spiritual Respect. This is the Old Red Road of Indian Spiritual Life. This is the Ancient Aboriginal Dreaming. This is the First Medicine Path of our People.

This is not a new age fling, nor are we talking about a fad or something that will come and go with wants and desires. We are sharing here a profoundly important initiation into the Mystery of Life, and that means we are Awakening to being Adults with Awareness, Consideration, and Conscience. We cannot as easily get away with all the easy mistakes of the past. We are called by the Spirit Fire into Sacred Accountability.

This means we are responsible to Carry the Dreaming, to Carry the Medicines on behalf of our Inner Spirit, on behalf of the People. We are called to become Custodians of the Earth World, just as much as many of us are called to Awaken the Sacred Duties of Medicine Men and Woman. Our paths in life demand we respect and honour these Ways.

You are reading these reflections for a reason unique to Your Path in Life. What do these Teachings say to you? What Awakens within Your Heart? What do you hear from Your Ancestors? What do they ask of You? Remember your journal and record your thoughts and feelings. Consider talking with a trusted Elder, friend, family member, or counsellor about your insights, questions, and concerns.

Remember that when our mind and heart are healthy and balanced, we will use our intuition and inner creativity to listen, look, and feel what is good and true. If your mental health is compromised in any way, like through depression or anxiety, or through forms of unstable thoughts and feelings, please know that you need to always bring your ideas and feelings to people you trust. Allow your family, friends and counsellors to help you discern the Ways of Spirit for your Life. We all need this help, and this is a big part of what our Ancestors wish for us - to be grounded and protected by our family, tribe and Nation. To be balanced and whole. M'sit No'koma. Ta'ho.

Joseph Randolph Bowers

March Siwkewiku's Spawning Moon

Pjila'si ~ Welcome, come in, sit down.

Siwkewiku's Spawning Moon brings stirrings of springtime even when the deep snows of winter persist. During this Moon let us honour the East and the Great Kitpu, Eagle Chief, who comes to us on the wings of change we do not see with our human eyes.

Even during this winter, we think of Eastern sunrises that bring warmer days. These days slowly grow longer. We need patience.

It should not surprise. Spawning Moon speaks of what happens in the World Beneath the Water. This is one of the Sacred Worlds of our Ancestors. So, we listen…

During this Moon our hearts listen... From the Deep Waters we long for insight from the Creator.

Great Eagle Chief flies above earth and water, and flies under earth and water. Great Kitpu Chief is messenger of Creator across the Sacred Worlds. So, we listen...

Kitpu brings memories from other times when our spirits are strong and brave. Let us call in this Medicine to walk in courage.

'Will my children return to the ways of the Sacred Pipe?' The Old Voice breaks through the cold, foggy haze. 'Tell my children that I am waiting.' Eagle Medicine certainly does wait until we are ready.

It seems to me that our modern world needs to listen... If so, many mainstream people seek the old ways, why do we Mi'kmaq rush into material life and put aside our culture, our spiritual ways? While we rush ahead, we can take our traditions with us to keep us strong. Everyone needs to slow down, sometime, somewhere.

Kitpu sings out, 'Tell my children the White Buffalo Calf is being born now among the People of the Eastern Door. Will they remember? Will they embrace all that was lost?'

Old Grandmothers remember many things... Lost medicine, lost culture, and lost children... All of whom are being reborn... The Seventh Generation is being born today...

And what about long-lost kin?

These children are from families who were separated from our People because of colonisation. Their Mi'kmaw parents married into Acadian and other families since the 1600s. They were systematically cut off from us by the Indian Act and other policies. Their children today carry the blood of our Ancestors. Their number gives us greater strength. No foreign power can destroy what God has brought together through marriage and blood.

The Grandmothers know it is true. The Grandmothers pray and sing for we who are being born today. The Ancestors see us as One Nation.

The children of the Seventh Generation are waking up. They instinctively know what many others have forgotten. The Sacred Medicines were protected for many moons. The Grandfathers know it is true. Something is awakening... Slowly opens the Eastern Door... Our role as People of the Dawn is coming back to us.

Reflection

We often think that listening is doing nothing. Listening is boring. Listening is a waste of time. These are often the thoughts of youth within us. We don't want or desire to listen. But the reality is, we need to listen. Listening is a basic human need. Listening is essential to survival. Listening is basic to all communication.

Learning to listen in conversation within relationships is the first step toward listening inwardly, to our intuition, feelings, and to spiritual insights. Listening in these ways keeps us protected during unsafe situations. Unless we listen and do something different, we could easily find ourselves in all kinds of trouble.

Listening is fundamental to respect. We respect ourselves when we know how to listen. If we don't know how, we respect our inner world by learning to listen. The first step is really simple: shut up! Stop talking all the time! Quiet your mind. Focus on one thing. Actually, focus on what someone else is saying. Put aside your thoughts that go, but, or yeah, I am thinking something else here, or go figure... We have all kinds of inner scripts. Listening is shutting up just long enough to actually hear what someone else is really saying.

But what does this mean? You have to experiment to learn. It might mean you stop and see how they say whatever they are saying. Maybe they have a bit of sarcasm, or humour, or anger, or fear. Maybe the words they say are not really what they mean. Maybe their body is doing something different. And maybe they are telling you something through their finger, or their legs, or their hips, or their shoulders. Watch them. This is part of listening too. Now it's getting tricky. By listening we actually mean to watch, look, and see what someone is really saying. Studies show as much as 98% of human communication is non-verbal. Now that is interesting.

Aboriginal people talk with their body. They dance, squirm, fart, get angry, throw a tantrum, laugh, hug, kiss, caress, pat each other's hair, and do all kinds of physical things with their bodies. We are a feeling people. Very often we are more in tune with our heart and feeling. Our languages tend to be more in touch with the Earth, and with Heart. We are Close to Spirit, and this means we are natural, and the Four Elements of Life are important to our feeling everything in Life.

We learn to really listen in our First Nation cultures. This is why we know the white fellah is often false, because we can see through people in the blink of an eye. Our eyes are not covered by lies and intellectual agendas. We see clearly. And we won't be fooled by words. But these are skills in life we learn, and we need to guard our hearts from being manipulated. We have been there before, and we know what it is like. We won't go there. We don't need to.

Ask yourself during this Sacred Moon tide, what do you really need in your life? Where do you need to listen more? And make a private, secret plan on how you will accomplish your turning that need into one of your strengths. In our weakness is our strength. In our need is our secret wisdom. M'sit No'koma. Ta'ho.

Joseph Randolph Bowers

Siwkw/Spring Moons

April Penatemuiku's Egg Laying Moon

Pjila'si ~ Welcome, come in, sit down.

During Penatemuiku's Egg Laying Moon the Powers of the East enter the Circle and grow in strength. Kitpu flies over the Eastern Waters and returns hope during our early springtime. New life comes to our People as life returns to our Mother.

During this Moon seeds left behind last year are beginning their journey. Sweet Grass burned from last year's harvest brings prayers of new promise. The Mourning Dove and Hummingbird get ready for their long migration back to Mi'kma'ki. The Moose, Deer and other grazing spirits grow more at-ease with the coming of new grass, new growth of fern, and other feed that will come in time.

Those who may not be forest types often come out to the edge of the wilderness this time of year. Their long winter stint pushes their spirits to reconnect. They might go for walks and explore nature once again. This moon brings great relief to Elders as well. The long nights of winter are mostly over. Promise of spring is close at hand.

No symbol makes more sense to me than Egg Laying Moon.

The Egg symbolises the cosmology of Mi'kmaw Sacred Worlds, reborn once again this time of year. Earth World lies at the heart of the Egg and is symbolised by Yellow Yoke. Yoke is the intensity of Sun rising in the Eastern Door. Our destiny as a People rests with our role as Wabanaki who guard the Eastern Door. All new life comes through the Yoke of the Egg, nourished by the fluids around this heart.

Around the Earth World of our People are the World Above the Earth, World Beneath the Earth, World Above the Water, and World Beneath the Water. Where the Egg rises like the tip of a triangle the higher realms lead to the World Above the Sky and all worlds are linked to the Spirit World which transcends and passes through all other places.

The Seven Sacred Directions are East, South, West, North, Above, Below, and Heart or Centre. Both the Sacred Worlds and Seven Directions are experiential. To understand these realities, we must walk the talk.

The link between the Worlds is the Sacred Doorpost of the Wigwam. The Doorpost is the Mi'kmaw symbol of the Ancient Shaman's Tree that links the Worlds and allows the Medicine Woman or Man to move between the Worlds to help those in need. The Wigwam is the Cosmic Egg – the womb of Mother Earth – the heart of family. Smoke rises through the top of Wigwam into the Spirit World all around and through the World Above the Earth to Creator who lives within all Worlds.

The Doorpost of the Wigwam supports the Door Covering. This passageway links inner family circles with outer communal circles and the many worlds beyond. The whole Cosmos is united in this way.

This cosmology or map of the universe links all things together. Oneness and harmony, conflict and change are all part of the Worlds of Our People. We give respect for constant change and great diversity in creation. We honour the Worlds of the Old Ones of the People. They give us a complete cosmology and philosophy. We have everything we need.

Reflection

A cosmology is a map of the world, not just an earth-map. A cosmology is a map of how the world(s) make sense, how they fit together. As we are discussing this, ask yourself what is your map of the universe? How does it all fit together? You likely have a sense of your world being your family, school, work, and your town or region. You might think about the natural world around you as part of your world. If you live in a city, you might think of your suburb or section of the city, the areas that surround, the places you go like the supermarket, and the wider city as a place you know. In a basic and true way, these examples are part of your cosmology.

If we think in a broader social and cultural way, a modern-day western cosmology will include the worlds of what we see, feel and touch as what is true. We rely on empirical evidence, quite often, to believe that something exists. For example, we know fire is hot. And we know that boiling water burns our skin. We believe these are empirical truths. They help to define our world. Our cosmology includes our physical world, the different properties of things, how they interact, and how we move about the world in a safe way.

Our cosmology may also include that the earth is a big ball, round and flies through space in an orbit around the sun. We may have cosmologies of the Milky Way as the solar system that centres around our sun, with its various planets that we may see in our imagination as part of our solar system. For example, I can often see Mars, Jupiter and Saturn because for some reason these planets colours and shapes stick out in my mind. Maybe this is because they are closer to the earth and are often photographed and images are often looked at when people talk about the stars. In any case, your cosmology may have different planets and other bodies that form a part of your universe.

People's cosmology also includes the worlds of feeling, sensation, and intuition. Cosmology may involve the world of dreams, visions and creative insights. For artists, a cosmology may centre on one's studio as a place of creation and work that gives life and meaning. Our cosmology can be deeply personal, as well as social and cultural.

Now you may understand why I talk about cosmology as part of Native beliefs and cultural values. Traditional Mi'kmaw cosmology was and remains a very complex and integral map of the universe and arose from the life and meaning of the People. When I talk about the Sacred Worlds of our traditional culture, I am referring to this cosmology. For us this view of the world is based in our experience and sharing our stories of our lives. In my personal Mi'kmaw cosmology there are many worlds that might not be a part of someone's life who lives in Bear River,

Nova Scotia. We may hold different views of the world based on our experiences. This does not mean we can't share our stories. Far from it. We do and often share our stories, because our worlds are enriched by listening to someone who is from a different place.

During this Sacred Moon time when the birds are laying their first eggs of spring, and when people are often beginning new projects, consider for yourself your cosmology and be aware that you are sowing a seed of something new. By asking these questions, and looking at your way of perceiving the world, you are learning to listen to yourself in new ways. You are also opening your heart and mind to learning new ways of re-mapping your world into a more Sacred and Connected Place. How you map your world relates to how you feel about your world. How do you want to change these things, so you have more inner resources? How do you wish to change these things, so you have more social resources? How can you share your world, your story, with others to enrich their world? Consider sketching, painting, or drawing an actual map of your world. What does it look like? If you are not a visual person, use small stones or sticks or natural things to symbolise your world. Take a picture of your world and post it on Facebook. Share your world with others... You may be surprised to learn your world is actually a very wonderful place. M'sit No'koma. Ta'ho.

Sacred Teachings

May Etqoljewiku's Frog-Croaking Moon

Pjila'si ~ Welcome, come in, sit down.

Etqoljewiku's Frog-croaking Moon is a time of great renewal through the Eastern Door. The Powers of the East are flowing freely as the Spring rains feed the May Flower, Fern, and first growth of Sweet Grass.

Welcome Eastern Door! Welcome Powers of the Wabanaki!

Why is the Sunrise our People's spiritual and cultural purpose? To understand this, my heart searches not in the obvious Earth World and World Above the Earth where the

Sun's energy is most felt. Rather I go into the World Beneath the Earth and seek out the Frog-People for insight and wisdom.

Once when I was cleaning up behind the house in Australia to set the foundation for a new deck, I found something very surprising. The area being dug out was surrounded by a concrete landing on all sides, left as dirt to support outdoor plants. The area was covered by a permanent roof. My intention was to fill in the floor and make an indoor-outdoor room.

In the hard-dry earth, I dug down about five feet into rock solid clay. It was hard work getting through. Sweaty and tired the shovel slipped just slightly. I pulled up the clay, went to throw it in the wheelbarrow, and stopped dead in my tracks.

Out of a hollow in the clay a small frog appeared. Shocked by the movement of the earth my little friend began to wake up.

In concern for my little brother, I rushed to get a bit of water. How long had my friend been in hibernation? It had been 36 years since the house was built, likely more than 25 years since this area had been disturbed and covered by a roof. This frog had lasted this long without food or water.

He slowly revived. In concern I left him in the now moist clay and placed him in a hollow of ground underneath a large log in the garden. Meantime I gave thanks to Creator with Tobacco. My shovel didn't harm Brother Frog. Thank you for this lesson today.

Ever since then my respect for frogs' verges on a mystical fascination. Frogs like Bears can hibernate for long periods. But I've never heard of a Bear staying in hibernation for 25 years!

Now while sitting in the back woods of Mi'kma'ki Brother Frog tells another tale. Spirit Frog seems to say, 'Learn about the sleep that preserves life. Learn about waking from hibernation. Tell my children they are waking up after a long winter. It is time their song was heard once again.'

The Wabanaki are People of the Dawn because we were destined to undergo a great and long trial, a draught of cultural assault, a very long winter over hundreds of years.

From the Underworld comes this lesson. From the darkness of the Sweat comes new light. From the Great Sleep of our People comes our Life-Giving Insight. From our Deepest Trauma comes our Courage and Strength.

We are Wabanaki. For us Brother Sun can only rise after a good long night of darkness. Father Sun goes down to Underworld to sleep. We sleep. Father Sun rises in Red Dawn. We rise. We rise before dawn to pray. In ceremony we are the First People of Turtle Island. We step into Great Mystery. New Birth. Our Strength. Who We Are.

Reflection

In a funny way, I often think of Frog Spirit as kin with Turtle Spirit, just without the hard shell on its back. I've never actually researched the relationships between frogs and turtles, but my intuition tells me they are kin in some way or other. Of course, we are all kin.

Why do I say this? Frog Spirit is a very Powerful Helper. During my life this Teaching grows in my heart slowly, over the years. Turtle Spirit is also a very Powerful Helper.

Both Frog and Turtle Spirit Nations give rise to Wisdom Teachings unique to their Totemic Powers. Connecting with these Energies is as simple as imagination, but I am also prone to feel that people are gifted by connections with the Spirit of an Entity like Frog or Turtle. This gift is given freely, but always for a purpose.

What does it mean to connect to a Spirit of an Entity of an Animal? For me, it feels like we connect with the Over-soul or Connective Spirit that Governs the Totemic Power or Territory of that Species. I am talking about experience in vision and prayer, and so these words come with difficulty, as describing the spiritual experience is not easy. Each Species has its own Energy Pattern. For me this comes into my senses like a feeling and a taste. Frog Spirit feels different from Turtle Spirit. These Spirits feel different from Wolf Spirit, etc. Each experience holds a 'taste' and I do not mean a taste in the mouth. I mean a complex 'flavour' that registers as part taste, part feeling, part colour, and part vibration. Because of my being a musician and painter, taste and sound are very interrelated to colour and feeling. These sensory systems work together.

This is part of the reason why it is so difficult to help others understand the experience of connecting with Totemic Powers. In the First Nation Way, we honour and seek connection with these Powers as our Kin. We feel this is an important part of our cosmology, our Map of Life. Every person relates to connecting with the Spirit of an Entity within Nature in different ways, through the sensory systems. Each person uses these systems in different ways. You need to explore, observe, and learn how your sense systems fit together. This will help you understand how you take in information, and how you are related to the world around you. This is knowledge no one else can give you. It is unique to you alone. But many people will experience their world in similar ways, which makes it interesting and fun to share our stories. We then hear, see and feel if not taste and smell how different people's worlds are from our own.

If you seek a connection with a Totemic Spirit, ask Creator to gift you with a new connection or to reveal to you an existing relationship. Very often most people I have met are already related to one or several Totemic Powers. They may have only overlooked or not understood what this means. Once you open your awareness to listening, looking and feeling something new, you may find that a creature, plant or animal, may come to you in your dreams, daydreams, or thoughts. You may see the animal or plant, or creature, in photographs or on TV or in the news. You may see the Entity in your daily life, a bird or snake or lizard or wolf. You may feel the connection in your heart without any evidence at all.

For example, my heart is deeply connected to the simple Daisy Spirit. In Australia the Paper Daisy comes to me in my dreams and appears in my artwork and imagery. I used this image for the cover of one of my recent books, *On the Threshold: Personal Transformation and Spiritual Awakening - A Primer on the Spiritual Life with Activities*. The Daisy Totem has so much to teach us in life. If only we would be open to listen with our inner ears, to look with our intuitive eyes, to feel with our passionate heart, and to learn with our deeply embedded and earth-grounded mind. I wish you every peace and blessing on this fascinating path to discovering and learning from your Totemic Powers. With all of our relations, I wish you every goodness. M'sit No'koma. Ta'ho.

June Nipniku's Summer Moon

Pjila'si ~ Welcome, come in, sit down.

During Nipniku's Summer Moon the Powers of the South rise higher. All the life of Father Sun comes forward toward the middle of the Sky World. The circle of family enters the medicine of Paq'tism Wolf-People who come through the Southern Door. During this moon we honour Elders and Grandparents who teach us the ways of nourishing family, caring for children, protecting our integrity and honour.

Many memories of my Grandmother Honora Richard-Bowers come to me this time of year. She took me into the woods, along the shore, and into the bush to admire and learn about the new plants rising up toward the sun. All through the year she collected berry and leaf from the Creator's garden. She taught us to never pick more than we need. We learned how to preserve food through the winter even during spring and summer moons. Her spirit carried a great respect for Creation.

When she passed over it felt like a whole culture was passing away. Our family was never the same again. But some of us grandchildren remember and pass on her wisdom. In this way her spirit lives on.

We can always learn from our Elders, Grandparents and those who passed over. In this way Aboriginal Peoples have a great resource that many other nations have forgotten.

Our Elders and Grandparents sit with Kitpu Eagle, Paq'tism Wolf, Muin Bear, and Migjigi Turtle, around the Medicine Wheel. Ketapekiewuksiek aq alasutmelsewuksiek – Singing for us and praying for us.

We too are called to sing and pray for our Elders, to carry the Medicines and Teachings they give to us. We are not asked to be overly protective of these Medicines and Teachings. What we carry belongs to Creator. What we are given we freely give. We learn a path of detachment. Letting go. New energy enters the Sacred Circle.

We are called to let go into freedom. We cannot hold on. We cannot control how things will unfold. We can offer subtle advice. We can give our prayers up to the Sacred Powers. At certain critical times we can act in ways that are right and true to our hearts. Then we let go again.

Control grows from fear. Fear grows from being hurt. Moving beyond these ways begins with love. Love grows from letting go. Letting go grows from small steps of trust. Trust grows from two paths. First, trust grows from giving a gift. Second, trust grows from embracing our hurt with understanding. Understanding and gift-giving grow from honour. Honour asks us to step up to a new challenge. Honour begins with honesty, truth, and justice. These grow from the goodness in our spirit and from life-long learning.

There was once a time when our families knew the freedom and natural solitude of the forests of Mi'kma'ki. For those who live in crowded places, the forest still exists. There is still a kind of balance we can live in today's world. One family will move into the bush. They will explore the balance. They will listen again. They will teach. From this one family the Mi'kmaq Nation will be reborn.

Reflection

Freedom is something greatly misunderstood in today's world. Youthful spirits think freedom is about choice to do this or that. Freedom is about having ability to buy things and do whatever you want with your time. Freedom is sought by people as a commodity. You can buy your own freedom, whether this means buying time or buying things or buying people to do whatever you want them to do. People think that this kind of freedom brings material success, and from this grows an ability to have influence, power and control over the world. In this worldview, freedom is not about bringing contentment because we always desire more. We learn to never be happy with what we have. To be happy and content is to admit death and defeat.

Sorry. This is not freedom. This is slavery to wants and desires.

Spiritual freedom is about having an inner part of the self, like the heart, that is completely free from being pulled or manipulated in any way.

Spiritual freedom is having an inner strength that stands alone, on its own feet, and cannot be swayed by other opinions or beliefs.

Spiritual freedom is being content with what you have right now, and with who you are in this very moment.

Contentment is not about accepting your circumstances, personality, or fate. Contentment is actually an attitude of Creation that lives within us when we are in-tune with our path in life. Contentment is how the flower looks to the sun. The flower is not trying to be anything else. The flower is itself. We are content when we are being true to our nature.

    Spiritual freedom is knowing the difference between my needs verses my wants and desires. I may want to eat out tonight because my stomach desires fast food. But my inner being knows I need a healthy meal tonight, because I had fast food last week and that is enough. If I eat fast food more than once a month my body starts collecting too much fat, and when I am fat, my lower back has more trouble carrying me around. In other ways my whole body is thrown out of balance. Fast food is a want and a desire - not a need.

    Spiritual freedom is understanding health boundaries and behaviour. In our modern world we are told we must seek absolute freedom, so we can do whatever we want to do. But the modern material and empirical world has little soul and even less heart. Every action has its equal in outcomes. We learn to be spiritually free by abiding by the Old Laws of our Ancestors that are in-tune with nature, our bodies, and our real needs in life. This means we are bound by ethics, morals and values. Our freedom comes from learning these dos and don'ts. When we choose to go a different way, we can't as easily fool ourselves into thinking we are exercising freedom. Making a choice and freedom are two quite different realities. People today confuse having choices with freedom.

    For instance, a man who chooses to disobey his inner conscience and abuses his wife financially and physically is making a choice to go against his own innate nature. He is going against the Old Laws of his People. Natural Law will eventually catch up to him in some external and powerful way. Inwardly, he already suffers spiritually due to his actions. His whole life is thrown out of balance. His relationship with his loved one is damaged. His status and place in his world and society is profoundly compromised. He has lost his sense of self-pride. He may fool himself. But spiritually balanced self-pride is based in an inner strength of character that can only come when we act with respect. Where do you place your spiritual freedom? M'sit No'koma. Ta'ho.

Sacred Teachings

Nipk/Summer Moons

July Peskewiku's Feather-shedding Moon

Pjila'si ~ Welcome, come in, sit down.

This is Peskewiku's Feather-shedding Moon and the Roman month of July. I sincerely hope no one reads my column this month because everyone is out enjoying the nice weather! Ha! There are so many good things to enjoy when Father Sun is high. In the fullness of the Southern Door remember to wear sunscreen. Too much of any good thing tips the balance. Protect your precious skin. Your skin keeps the good parts in! Ha!

This moon I want to shed some old feathers and dance the old Two Spirited way. Just a little different from my brothers and sisters. Kisiku awakens and wishes to dance with my sister grandmothers, to enjoy our being old enough that we no longer care too much what other people say! We might still have the wolverine in us yet!

Oddly enough now is winter where I live in Australia. We are busy teaching counselling students who come from across the country for four-day intensives. They learn skills of communication, and strategies in helping people solve their problems. They learn about healing and how to help others cope with the pressures of today. There are many ways to dance... Isn't it amazing how the seasons are polar opposite between Australia and Mi'kma'ki?! Summer is winter. Winter is summer. Autumn is spring. Spring is autumn. This radical experience teaches me so much. Helps me to dance in new ways.

Creator asks us to leave the familiar to gain new perspectives. This is why we enter Sweat Lodge Ceremony. We change our body-environment to shift our mind-space. This opens new spiritual perception. Taking a Spirit Walk takes many forms. We listen to Sound of Drum. Heartbeat of Mother. This Sound carries us safely across Sacred Worlds. Sometimes Creator calls us to become Whale People. Other times Beaver Medicine. Sometimes Creator brings us to a New Place.

When Creator showed me vision of an Old Red Dirt Country very different from Red Dirt Mi'kma'ki, I did not know about Australia. Only later circumstances changed, new pathways opened. Suddenly I was part of an Australian Aboriginal family! Suddenly my life changed forever.

New Spirit People came to help me in my work. Kangaroo stood tall over me one day after work, 'Welcome to Country' he said to me. His eyes searched my soul. The silence enveloped my whole body. That stopped me in my tracks, wow.

Koala People met me at night, looking down at me from the eucalyptus trees. 'Welcome to Country!' They said. My heart was delighted to meet their acquaintance! Brother and Sister People in human form from my new Aboriginal family of Nations welcomed me too. Their Elders challenged me to reconnect with the Mi'kmaw in me. They celebrated my Aboriginal spirit. They asked me to step up to new honour, new responsibility. They told me the Eagle Spirit would go ahead of me during my visit back home. New doors would open up. It was true, beyond my wildest dreams.

Taking pride in who we are can grow in us regardless how far away from home we are. How far away we feel. Our Mi'kmaw ways are Mother Earth's teachings. The humility it takes to learn these ways is profound. I am more humbled every day. Let us dance during the Powwow with new energy. Be true to who you are.

Reflection

One of our Elders saw that certain birds shed their feathers during this moon. The summer moons hold much strength for letting go of things, and this gives us the energy to grow new wings. What do you need to let go of now? What can you be parted with?

Consider dusting out the cobwebs and seeing what you really need to keep verses what you can give away. This is also the month when many of our People gather and celebrate the Give Away Ceremony. This is a time to give many items to others that we no longer need to carry around or keep in our homes. Warm weather and summer hold a Spirit of Generosity that is innate to the Mi'kmaq People. We give from what we have. This is the Old Way.

Joseph Randolph Bowers

There is an important ethical and moral teaching about giving. Don't give what is easy for you to give. That holds very little reward for you. Instead, give what is most difficult to let go of. What do you treasure? Find your precious item and give it away.

Don't just give it to your loved one so that you keep that treasure closer to yourself. Give that precious item to someone more distant to you, a friend or acquaintance. If you really want an inner spiritual freedom, give that item to a more distant person or a stranger, or to your enemy. Then you will know inner freedom. M'sit No'koma. Ta'ho.

Sacred Teachings

August Kisikwekewiku's Fruit and Berry-Ripening Moon

Pjila'si ~ Welcome, come in, sit down.

What moon gives us many fruits and berries ripening on trees and bushes? Think hard now... You got it right! It is Kisikwekewiku's Fruit and Berry-Ripening Moon! We intuit the energies of the Western Door rising during this moon... The fullness of the berries, ripening of projects undertaken, and wisdom gained from all the experiences of this year speak of Elder energy awakening as the Western Spirits enter the circle.

For a long time, I thought the Mi'kmaq Maliseet Nations News ought to put the Mi'kmaw moon names in each issue instead of the Roman names. It seemed to me like they ought to help teach the People these themes for each moon.

Then I realised that these themes are very important in my work and my life. Each moon now my heart is renewed in strength by sitting to reflect on the spirit and teaching of that moon-time. Each moon my heart is healed just a little bit more by writing these reflections and sharing them with friends.

Kisiku says to me, 'With a good heart we can learn so much. Creator wants all Mi'kmaq children of all ages to celebrate their learning and growth.' She speaks strong and straight like an arrow.

During Kisikwekewiku Moon, Elders placed a most sacred gift into my hands. The gift brought many tears of joy. I was overwhelmed. Grandmother helped me tenderly and held me while I sobbed. A feeling of humility broke open my heart.

Sometimes Creator wants to break into our hearts so passionately, so deeply. We will either go with the flow or make ourselves sick. This time I decided to go with the flow. God knows for many years I made myself sick. Not now. Creator taught me too much over these years. Now Father Sun has me on the Red Path of honour. Now Grandmother Moon has me learning the ways of Medicine Teachings.

Into that space opened up by an empty heart came a new Spirit Person. Helper. Guide. Healer. Messenger. Teacher. What a surprising revelation!

This moon my heart wishes to say thank you dearest Elders for trusting Creator. Thank you for your love and friendship. Wela'lin each one. You know my love. You know my prayers come through big smoke through the heart of Mother Earth from a distant Aboriginal country. Wela'lin to your hearts of golden light. Your stars shine in the darkness and forever give light to the Southern Door.

This moon let us remember the Treaties of Peace and Friendship. Let us continue to show the Canadian mainstream that we are strong and proud People. Let us continue to offer an open hand of invitation. This is our way. This is who we are.

Reflection

This Sacred Moon tide gives much blessings. During this time of the year we are filling up with the goodness from the natural world around us. This brings the Spirit of the Give Away to the foreground. Consider during this New Moon ways you can offer hospitality. Remember those who are less fortunate than you and consider people who are poor and need resources that you can share.

Spirituality is about social and environmental justice. The most powerful social movements through the centuries across all cultures have been motivated by deeply felt spiritual truths. People seek justice. People wish to protect the environment. People seek equality and fairness. All the major revolutions have happened due to these very issues.

Remember that your giving might simply be a gift of time. Sit with your Elders. Listen to them. Make your parent's life a bit easier, do something helpful for them. Give your brother or your sister a thoughtful gift you know they will enjoy and give it some thought. Don't just spin in your wheels. Do something people will remember as kind and generous and will make a memory for them they will cherish for years to come. M'sit No'koma. Ta'ho.

Joseph Randolph Bowers

September Wikumkewiku's Moose-calling Moon

Pjila'si ~ Welcome, come in, sit down.

We move into the Western Door during this time of year as the fullness of the seasons come together in these next two harvest moons. We are now enjoying Wikumkewiku's Moose-calling Moon, a very special time for the Mi'kmaq People. Traditional foods and medicines are greatly enjoyed this time of year as we prepare to gather, hunt, and preserve our meats and many other foods for a long winter ahead.

Funny enough in today's world for those of us who take the powwow trail, and for many others who dive into summer's high energy activities, this moon can sometimes be a bit of a down time. Personally, I like a break during this moon to ponder the year gone by and to set my sights on what lies ahead. Autumn to come for me is always time to make major changes and set things in motion for the future. My spirit remembers the quickening brought about by the turning leaves. My dad's spirit was always excited this time of year as he made preparations and got ready for the autumn hunt. We often benefited all through the winter with the game he brought home this time of year.

Just as funny is how my spirit starts to get more focused-on family this time of year. My hands instinctively take up the crochet hook and start making crafts as the evening light fades. Nanny taught me to crochet and I've enjoyed it as a way to pray and give to others. She taught me that gifts made during the next three moons are given to loved ones during the long winter when people need a kind word and a special surprise.

Nanny and dad got us kids together through the autumn to do crafts in the evening. We started preparing for crafts in this moon by gathering natural resources from the forest or seaside, or by shopping in the stores. Doing this in a focused way in this moon taught us a great skill. Later on, we started putting aside resources all year. We were old enough to anticipate these moons, knowing that this special time of productivity and our family circle of making crafts would come around again.

You might be interested to know. Autumn traditions like these are part of Maritime Canadian and Aboriginal culture that are unique around the globe. Living overseas my instinct still remains true to our climate and culture here in Mi'kma'ki. Even when the sun is rising higher this time of year and summer is coming around in Australia, my body wants to home-in, get ready for winter, and start making crafts! It's too funny! People think I am quite strange! But it's taken me ten years to make some compromises with the local climate and customs to find a path that is good for me in respect for my heritage and identity.

These experiences of living and working in Australia deepen appreciation for how unique and precious our traditions really are. Giving back my work to the Mi'kmaq Resource Centre at Cape Breton University makes the circle complete because through the year our traditions of making resources to give to others continues even through writing, research, and teaching in the mainstream university system. Our lives are not our own. We exist because our Ancestors worked hard to give us life. What we do and make today is for our children and for the Seventh Generation we will not meet face to face in this time.

Reflection

Take note during this New Moon what your important family traditions have been. As the summer moons are coming to an end, remember that autumn holds a time of change that lies ahead. What new traditions might you like to celebrate this coming season? Maybe you will consider using the same tradition but in a new way?

For example, my father grew up in a rather poor family. He was the oldest of eight. He felt responsible early on, and left school to find work to help feed his brothers and sisters. Later in life, he put himself through night school. Eventually he became an Engineer and was highly regarded in his field of practice. When he had children of his own, he decided that making crafts and planning to celebrate the winter season was important to pass on to his children. When we were old enough, he always took out the Christmas tree lights during late September or early October. My birthday was this time of year, and so he made it a tradition to start planning for the Christmas holiday around the turn of the season.

As we grew up, we were charged with making decorations and gifts for others and for our house. We made some amazing things over the years. Our Grandmother's heritage was deeply influenced by growing up in the countryside along the Eastern Shore of Nova Scotia, with her French Acadian and Mi'kmaw heritage. My father got a lot of his traits from her, including his dark skin and deep brown eyes. Our Grandmother came to visit during the autumn moons and taught us much about doing crafts, making things, and putting our time to good use during the lengthening evenings in Canada.

There is little doubt that my father's revision of traditions took many Old Ways and brought them into our family context, translated them into things we could do together, and made sense to our daily life. These experiences taught us self-reliance, creativity, problem solving, planning for something to come, collecting resources from nature, skills of patience, endurance, and generosity, to name a few. These experiences provided our Grandmother a time to share her wisdom. We did not know then, but my father was aware of our Grandmother's influence. She carried the Old Ways including many memories, stories and experiences. Those years with her were some of the most important of my life. What traditions do you wish to create or revise for yourself and your children? M'sit No'koma. Ta'ho.

Joseph Randolph Bowers

Toqa'q/Autumn Moons

October Wikewiku's Animal-fattening Moon

Pjila'si ~ Welcome, come in, sit down.

Welcome to Wikewiku's Animal-fattening Moon! This is surely my favourite time of year! In this moon the leaves turn spectacular colours. Many leaves and berries are ripe for picking. The Western Door opens with intensity so that Elder wisdom can be accessed more easily. Our Ancestors wish to come into the circle even more this time of year. Their voices are easier to hear. The doorways between the Worlds are more easily tracked.

My spirit is happiest this time of year, for sure. Everyone seems a good busy getting ready for winter. Family time starts to grow longer as the sunlight fades and evenings grow longer. This really means the world to me.

Being a Western Door kind of personality, this moon always brings me to honour Ancestors and remember those who have passed to the other Worlds. This time of year, a visit to resting places of our People restores my peace. Bringing offerings always makes my heart settle. If our People today forget these old ways life will get harder for future generations. Keeping things in balance is a path of humility, honour, and respect.

Teaching kids these traditions start with sharing basic customs. Visiting resting places of our family members who passed on is difficult for some folks but is important. Caring for these places is also important. Usually one of the kids will seem more in tune with these responsibilities. They might come to carry these traditions into the next generation. But to find those children means that all the children need to be taught from an early age to respect and care for the Ancestors.

Many remember offering a sample of best food from each dinner to the Ancestors. The food is often placed in a fire as an offering, practical with many animals around who would be attracted by the smell of food. In Australia food is left out for relations who are tracking in the bush. Many leave food at the edge of town for those who are still living the old ways. Whether they are in flesh or spirit is the same thing – it all comes down to respect.

Those who carry Sacred Pipes play a part in caring for the Ancestors. The family, group, and nation Pipe are like a welcome wigwam, a place of gathering. In this space peace and friendship are promoted by remembering basic values of respect, honour, trust, forgiveness, humility, humour, and responsibility. These values invite the Old Ones of the People into community with us today. We who are in our skin-time are only one step away from them. We need to pay respect.

The gathering Pipes of our families, communities, and the Mi'kmaq Nation Pipes call those who believe and those who wish to respect other's beliefs to a place of honour. With honour comes respect and responsibility. These are practiced with humility. Through these qualities we can learn the ways of forgiveness, humour, and trust. These pathways are given to us from our Ancestors and from the White Buffalo Calf Woman who gave us the Sacred Pipe.

We need to remember who we are. The Pipe wishes us to acknowledge. Acknowledgement for the Mi'kmaq People is really important. To acknowledge means to affirm, support, encourage, and feel pride in who we are. To walk in strength in our own communities, and without fear.

Reflection

Take this Sacred New Moon time to offer respect for your family through those who have passed on. Remember a family member who fought in war so that you might live a better life. Take time out to visit a cemetery and bring flowers or some other offering with you to place on a grave. Perhaps you might even go into a cemetery where your family is not buried - with the intention to pay respect to other people's family. Bring flowers and place them on a grave where there are none, or where the grave is very simple and without decoration.

Consider lighting a tea candle in a safe candle-glass and burn this candle for your Grandmother or Grandfather. Place flowers by their picture. It does not matter if they are alive or passed over. Either way, the candle brings a spirit of prayerful thanksgiving and wishing them well. Write in your journal the meaning of these actions for you, and things that you may learn through your experience. M'sit No'koma, Ta'ho.

November Keptekewiku's River-freezing Moon

Pjila'si ~ Welcome, come in, sit down.

During Keptekewiku's River-freezing Moon the energy of the Northern Door is rising. Grandmothers and Grandfathers of the North, welcome to our circle. In places like Australia, from the North comes the heat of Father Sun and longer days. In Mi'kma'ki, Father Sun recedes to the far sky and our days grow short. In either place I appreciate Grandmother Turtle and remember the original Clan Mothers from which all two-legged were created.

In Keptekewiku's moon we can appreciate the Eastern Door each day. Welcome Brother Sun! We Old Souls make a little sacrifice of sleep to worship Creator before the rising of the sun. Today this is a good discipline for the young ones to experience. A little sacrifice goes a long way. Eagle Medicine is in this Eastern Door ready for us whenever we come to worship and give thanks. Welcome Kitpu'skw! We need your guidance now!

Across the sky, in the Western Door, we feel energy to help us complete the projects undertaken during the Autumn moons. Muin'skw is Mother Bear of all our projects. She protects us, gives us energy, and moves us forward during this dark time of year. Her smoke rising from the Den is a sure sign of things to come.

In Keptekewiku's Moon we are inside the time of family.

The evenings and weekends are opportunities for family games, crafts, and relaxing time around the television or listening to music. This is a great time to enjoy drumming circles. This is also a great time to seek quiet and prayer, to engage in personal or familial ceremony, and to deepen our spirituality through reading, listening or learning.

This time of year is a great opportunity for Mi'kmaq families to restore the goodness of family life. Restoring the family circle is a sacred and practical task. Children depend on strong family relations to help them gain the skills they need for life and living.

In today's world all cultures are challenged to keep a focus on family. We Aboriginal people are no different in this regard.

Reflection

During this Moon time plan a new activity, something you have never done before. If you don't have a list of things you want to do, but never seem to get time for, make that list now. Pick one of the items and decide to just do it. You may want to include your family.

Another idea is to learn a new craft. This may take a little preparation. Visit a craft store or seek information on the internet. Choose something you will enjoy. One year I collected large pinecones, and then painted them with nail polish. It was something fun to do with family, and we gave the pinecones to people at Christmas.

If these ideas seem weird, pick a new game you can learn with your family. Maybe get over a computer phobia and learn a computer game. So often the computer takes family members away from each other. Well, why not turn that around and find games that need more than one person.

Let your journal reflections be about social events that you can enjoy. Make note of how other people react. Use this information to help you plan future fun activities. M'sit No'koma. Ta'ho.

Joseph Randolph Bowers

December Kjiku's The Great Moon

Pjila'si ~ Welcome, come in, sit down.

This is Kjiku's The Great Moon. During this moon my Elders teach me to listen to the quiet snow resting on the limbs of trees. My Grandmother taught me to bundle up nice and warm and sit in the deep forest during this moon. She showed me how to find a place of peace inside my being – a place where mind, heart, and spirit are one. She helped me find that place through my breath.
When you sit in the cold you see your breath. When you really sit and ponder, you have powerful meditation. Your breath is your life. Your life is Creator's gift. Every breath is clearly visible. The cold of winter reminds us to be aware of our breathing. We need clean air, clean water, and clean thoughts. If

any of these three are mud, we start to lose our path. Our health starts to fail. We need to find our breath. This is the way back to our original balance – the balance our Grandmothers teach us.

In this moon my Nanny taught me to think clean thoughts. From my breath, she showed me the place of inner tranquillity. Then she showed me the peace of the woods around me. I observed with her. We stayed there for many hours, watching the snow on the limbs of trees. In the cold we sat. Under the spruce, silver birch, and fir tree.

In my inner place I remember the Salmon jumping up the river in moons past. Then Nanny gave me these words for a poem:

Salmon don't swim against the stream.
They swim with the stream.
In the stream, they are in the stream.
That is the message.
Two legged are on the path or like fish out of water.
When you lose your path, find it, and jump back in.
Is this destiny, or just staying out of trouble?
Only the salmon know.

We are the only creature that can consciously choose to step off our path in life, to destroy our habitat and food source, and to upset the delicate balance that sustains our co-existence with our environment.

The Native Peoples always knew of this human destructive power. That is why they put in place very strong ethical and social laws that govern our relations with all other sentient and non-sentient creatures. These laws go with the flow of non-interference and respect for what life brings. This way bases our progress in balanced relations with all of life around us – in deep ethical principles that guide our actions. Sometimes we may choose to not benefit personally because we respect other interests are equally important to consider.

Let us pray for a little more wisdom during the year ahead. Let us remember our breath. We can pray, let my path find me. Let me stop doing all the work. Let me stop thinking I can do any of the work myself. Let me rely on Creator in humility. Let my life speak without speaking.

Reflection

Congratulate yourself. You have already read and perhaps also practiced the Moon tides for two yearly cycles. Your doing this shows a huge degree of personal commitment and a great deal of learning.

Take this New Moon to open yourself to all of the collective learning engaged over these two years. Do a review of your journals and begin from day one when you started this book. Skim through the pages of your journal and read the bits that stand out to you. Observe the ways that your perspectives changed, or that your feelings toward life altered in some way or other.

As you move toward the Full Moon during the end of this year, plan a personal celebration for yourself. Do something empowering for you. Even if that is as simple as lighting a candle for your inner Spirit. M'sit No'koma. Ta'ho.

Sacred Teachings

The Third Moon Cycle: Year Three

Joseph Randolph Bowers

Kesik/Winter Moons

January Punamujuiku's Frost Fish Moon

Pjila'si ~ Welcome, come in, sit down and share the warmth of this Sacred Fire.

Last year we introduced the feeling of how the Sacred Moons have teachings for us that help us on our walk. We learned that cultural wisdom has great utility in today's world. We honoured our Elders and Ancestors for all they have given to us. During the moon cycles of last year my heart sought the wisdom of the Medicine Wheel.

More and more, little insights came through times of retreat from a busy life. A deeper stillness was given after times of sweat and tears. Isn't this an inspiring story? We can in our day re-learn the teachings of our Ancestors. These ways are embedded in our blood and come through our dreaming.

With a deepening feeling of humility, let me say that Mi'kmaq Elders and the Editor of the Mi'kmaq Maliseet Nations News asked me to continue writing. My response was surely someone else can do this work better than myself. But they asked. For many personal reasons their advice is hard to carry out. Their words are good and true.

Under the spectacular Southern Door, looking for many nights upon the array of stars streaming across the sky, it came to me that my Elder's words bring me to walk the pathway of our Ancestors. The Milky Way can be seen with great clarity standing under the constellation of the Black Swan of Australia. What is hidden to the wise, children often know.

Each time... A deeper responsibility. In sitting through the darkness with a good spirit helper, gifts will come to those whose heart and mind are ready to listen. Like everything on the Good Red Road of Indian spirituality, take what is useful for you and disregard the rest. When you consider the complete expanse of the stars, you can only be reminded of the Medicine Wheel of Life for Our People. The Medicine Wheel is like a map of the constellations and can become our Primary Teacher in ways of health and wellbeing. A knowledge not new to us. A knowing as old as the stars whose light shines with the power of our Ancestor's spirits. This is true because we re-learn parts of our identity. Parts of ourselves come back to us through the Seventh Generation.

We are the stars who sing. Our song is our light. This ancient song of our Elders is awakening once again. In the fire of our living tradition, the story is tested. Seek the Elders. Ask them for advice. Open your heart. Seek your own healing. This is the power within us to create worlds and to destroy worlds. We are a powerful people. Healing is within our being. This is who we are. Follow your heart. Eagle Medicine wishes the Mi'kmaq Nation to know that Our Medicine Wheel is our path to health and wellbeing. Our source of life. Our path of healing and power.

Kwe, greetings. We acknowledge Punamujuiku's Frost Fish Moon. This moon sits in the Powers of the North. In the North sits Migjigi – Turtle People, who govern the Sacred Medicines of Our People. Migjigi have much to teach us. Migjigi are a Great People. They are our Elders and Ancient Ancestors whose wisdom governs all our lives. They are Mother and Grandmother, because on the back of the Turtle we have life. She is our Mother Earth. The thirteen sections you find on the Turtle's back are the original Mothers who gave birth to the tribes of humanity. This birthing is still happening. If you listen closely, you can still hear them singing for this generation. They are singing right now for you. Just listen... You will hear them. Raise your Sacred Pipes in Unison. Smoke for our Mothers.

Reflection

Imagine the Grandmothers are singing to you. What do they sing? What would they wish you to know?

Focus on this message. This is your Medicine for this coming year. M'sit No'koma. Ta'ho.

Sacred Teachings

February Apiknajit Snow Blinder Moon

Pjila'si ~ Welcome, come in, sit down.

In this Sacred Moon of Winter, Apiknajit Snow Blinder Moon is a time to honour the Sacred Medicine of Water through the Sacred Herb of Tobacco smoked under the heavy-laden branches of the Pines and other Sacred Herb trees of Our Land. The Sacred Colour for the Winter Moon Cycle is white. In Australia white ochre is painted on our faces during the mourning cries. White represents our Ancestors and those who have passed over. In Mi'kma'ki white is a colour representing Elder wisdom, because when we grow into this life-stage our hair turns white. For many Aboriginal Nations white is the colour of the Great Spirit.

This is an important Medicine Teaching for today. In today's world we Aboriginal Nations risk letting go of our spirits by walking the path of materialism and other European philosophies that offer a way to separate the people from the land. During the industrial revolution in Europe, these ways of thinking dominated all walks of life, and further diminished ancient European tribal wisdom. The politics of how we think is critically important. How we think manifests into how we live. How we live creates our world, for better or for worse. This is our Power to manifest. We use it with great care.

Apiknajit Moon is an important time because this is when the White Bear commands the lands of the North. We pray for the health and survival of the Bear People in the North. We raise the Sacred Pipes of our Nation. Ta'ho.

Our helpers in this moon wish us to know. We can enjoy the things of this world. We can also have clean hearts. We can be detached from what we have and what we enjoy. We can walk away from wealth. We can give wealth away. We can receive wealth for the good of others. We can live in the spirit of the Long House time of our People when we shared everything in common. We can hold the white man's deeds to land, but still place this Our Sacred Land under legal ecological protection and perpetual covenants that allow all our People access and use of the land's resources. We can walk in a humble way in a world of great knowledge and learning. We can even present our culture on-line to the global community and stand proud in our heritage. We are truly an amazing People.

We can feel the intense power and integrity of the Wampum. We can be overwhelmed by the Sacred Presence, and after a very long and hard walk we can know that we are finally home.

We pray especially for those who survived the residential schools. These members of our community may carry terrible and traumatic memories from their past winters. This may be an especially lonely and difficult time. We pray for their strength and healing.

We younger ones also carry the trauma and healing of our parent's parents. It is our way. It is who we are. We carry the burdens of our Elders, our Ancestors, and our Ancient Land. Our Elders need our youthful strength during these Winter Moons. We are all on a path of healing and restoration of our dignity.

Reflection

During the New Moon, if your heart is so called, burn a white candle for the Elders of the Mi'kmaq Nation. In this book I have asked you nothing for myself or for my People. In this Moon, burn a candle for our Elders, especially those who carry the Traditions and Wisdom-Memories to the new generation. They need your help and support. They are a faithful group of our People who dedicate their lives to serving others with humility, and with pride of heart for our children.

In my life, I have travelled all around the world many times. Because of living in Australia, Mi'kma'ki is literally 18,000 miles for me one way - half the circumference of the Sacred Earth. For that reason, when I travel back home, I often take the 'round the world' flight packages. At times I have visited the Orient, Europe, the Americas, and the Pacific region. Wherever I have gone, in my heart I have never met a People so deeply moving and respected as the Mi'kmaq Nation.

Thank you for your prayers. Our Elders have much to offer the world. They have always been around when the world has been suffering. Their cultural knowledge and teachings are rich and powerful. They often give of their hearts without any notice to the personal cost. They are a generous, open hearted and giving People. They live by example. And they walk the Red Road of Indian spirituality without praise or hype or with seeking any social recognition. They teach that anyone who claims to be an Elder is a false teacher, and they are right. The true Medicine Person lives their calling in their work and does not seek attention. It is a rare human being who gives away what they have without seeking some form of payment or reward.

In the Old Ways of the People, our culture was itself the environment that made living these Ways possible and sustainable. When everyone has the same or similar values, people who carry Medicines can offer their worth for 'free' because the members of the tribe offered the Elders gifts of food, shelter, assistance in gathering food, and all that they needed to live a comfortable life. People were provided for from whatever the People shared. If you had a gift, you shared it with others from a heart filled with gratitude. No one was wanting.

In today's world the Old Ways are still highly respected. And the challenges to live that Way even greater, because not everyone lives in this worldview. Not everyone lives from a place of service to others. Selfishness, greed, fear and self-protective spirits have come into the tribe and often dominate with the petty spirit of alcohol. This greatly diminishes the People's capacity to survive and thrive.

This makes it so very challenging for the Elders who still walk the Red Road. They often must give but no one gives them any help or assistance. The Medicine Elders are often left with very little to survive. They become lonely, isolated, without personal resources to survive and hungry for lack of healthy and good food.

Therefore, if and when you ever seek out and visit a Native or Aboriginal Elder, always bring them a bag of food as a respect offering. Many First Nation Elders appreciate a package of Tobacco, offered to their Sacred Pipe, if you are aware, they carry such Medicine. Food, tobacco and some money are highly appreciated. Fifty or sixty dollars would be greatly appreciated.

These offerings can be given in such a way as to not draw attention to the value of the gifts, but to place the offerings on a table or someplace the Elder can access them if they choose to open them when you are present. In some cultures it is appropriate to offer the gifts directly and place them in the hands of the Elder. If you are not sure, ask people first.

Many of our Elders who have a genuine heart would say, oh no, that is too much for me, and give much of what you offer back before accepting the gifts. This is their way to show humility and caring for your wellbeing. You then have the choice of offering the gifts again, and insisting they accept them with a sign of your willingness to give with a heart of love. They will very likely see your inner motivations by the way you offer a gift. Thank you again for considering our Elders. M'sit No'koma. Ta'ho.

Joseph Randolph Bowers

March Siwkewiku's Spawning Moon

Pjila'si ~ Welcome, come in, sit down.

Let me share a story. One night in the winter moon my heart got full. Eagle Medicine asked me to pray. In my simple way, I prepared the Medicines. Sage from Turtle Island gave me strength and purified my body to stand in the Sacred Presence of Great Medicine. Praying under the spirit of the Black Swan (the star formation above Australia, called the Southern Cross by Europeans), I was reminded of teachings given to me about the Milky Way.

The Milky Way, my Grandmother once told me, is the highway of the Spirits where those who pass over will go to meet All Our Relations. This is the place of restoration of strength, renewal, and preparation for the next walk. The Star World is the Summer Place that dwells in the South, where the Sun's heat reaches a fullness of blessings.

As my eyes looked up, the Milky Way stretched from the South above the Pines to the North above the Gums. Beginning in the North, I honoured the Turtle People, our Ancestors and Clan Mothers. In my heart they said to me, 'Take it slow. Steady. One step at a time.' Prayers for the Mi'kmaq Nation and our Elders entered the Sacred Pipe.

Turning to the East, honouring Eagle Nation, heart bending low in humility. Offering of Sacred Tobacco to Mother Earth for the Spirit of the Pipe. Give us strength and clarity of vision, hearts strong and brave. Open our minds to look, and feet steady to walk the way of warriors for peace. Prayers for the healing of the Land entered the Sacred Pipe.

In the South Paq'tism – Wolf People ran ahead of me, telling me immediately they would prepare a way for us, they would test that way first, to make sure the way is safe. When we see the Alpha Paq'tism coming, we will know the way is clear. Prayers for all our plans, for new projects, and for our Nation's prosperity and future entered the Sacred Pipe.

Toward the West, the Great Bear People showed us a vision. They walked through a very thick forest. They cleared a path as they went. The moon was high, and full. They found a special place there, in the deep of the quiet places. They started felling some trees and made a place of refuge. Then I realised they were preparing for a long winter ahead. The Mother of the Bear People said, 'We will protect you when you need shelter the most. We will go to the Dreaming Places. With your forefathers, we will open the way and protect your work.' Prayers for our mothers and fathers, and for the political leaders of our people, entered the Sacred Pipe.

That night many more prayers were offered up to Creator's heart song. Across the Worlds and along the pathway of the stars, the smoke of our lives is given to those we love in this skin-time, and to those who are in spirit.

During Siwkewiku's Spawning Moon something new is happening among our People. This moon marks the beginning of the life cycle of childhood. We are remembering who we are and finding new ways to honour our traditions in today's contemporary world. We are taking up the challenges, learning the songs, reclaiming our language. We are giving hope to our Elders, supporting our parents, and working hard to keep up in school so we can better the future of our People. Let us sing the Honour Song and feel rich and full of heart. We are a proud People. We walk in humility. We know who we are.

Reflection

This Moon tide reminds me of the things that cling to us, and the things that are letting go. Winter hangs on like an old coat. But signs of spring are coming. The Earth is ready for a change. Our bodies are tired after a long winter. So often we have no rest during the winter, and we are expected by our jobs and responsibilities to continue the crazy pace of life.

Mainstream Canadian, American and Australian cultures are work-driven and economically possessed of heart and mind. The system is set up so that no one except the very rich ever have leisure time to enjoy the bounty of life and work. In the Old Days, people used to sit by the fire during winter and share stories. Women would do needle work, crochet, and make blankets, clothing and other items useful for life. Men would read, play music, and make wood craft. Children would learn the ways of craft and social play from their older siblings and parents. Young ones would learn to cook, and to work with the preserves of meat, fish and vegetables. Many life-skills were learned during the long winter moons.

Consider during this Moon how you can make your children's lives a bit easier and less work driven. Put aside funds to buy a home, and pay off the mortgage, so you will have something to pass on to your children and grandchildren. Make a plan for their future education expenses. Even a small amount of money put aside can make a huge difference in years to come. Look into forms of long-term education savings plans. Perhaps you will find a way to increase your family's wealth and prosperity.

Spiritual visions often have very practical implications. In the real world of people, places and things, we need resources to survive and to thrive. Political powers understand this wisdom. They chose to possess the land and take it from our Ancestors. This is why they refuse to honour the Treaties that allowed their kin to stay in our territories. We never gave the land away. We never sold the land. And we never gave up rights to the land. But this is the main resource that is claimed by present day governments. Their wealth and power are gained at the expense of Aboriginal Nations who now live in poverty and in Fourth World conditions. Remember with humility that the spirituality you seek has practical, worldly and political implications. When your spiritual life is true, it will give you strength to face the challenges ahead with integrity and peace of heart. Remember also. First Nation spirituality is real, down to earth, and practical. We stand by our Teachings. They make sense. They are deep-feeling and have political weight. The Original Teachings guide everything in life. M'sit No'koma. Ta'ho.

Joseph Randolph Bowers

Siwkw/Spring Moons

April Penatemuiku's Egg Laying Moon

Pjila'si ~ Welcome, come in, sit down.

Let me share teachings that come to me from Eagle Medicine about the Sacred Medicine Wheel of our People. As we move around the Sacred Circle of the year, we also come to know the Four Sacred Directions of our Medicine Wheel. Each of the Four Cardinal Directions includes three Sacred Moons.

Sacred Teachings

Last month we entered the life cycle of the Child who sits in the East.

The colour of the East is Yellow where the Sun rises over the Wabanaki. The Sacred Element is Earth from which the child receives life. The Sacred Herb is Sweet Grass that rises through the Earth to the Sun during these Spring Moons. There are many teachings that arise from the Sacred Medicine Wheel.

An Elder shared with me that each person's knowledge of the Sacred Wheel is unique and to be respected. There are common aspects, and many variations. Each Cardinal Direction brings in Helpers. The Eagle Medicine Pipe celebrates the Bald Eagle in the East. Kitpu, Eagle governs this sacred direction and characterises the spirit of our people.

When Eagle Medicine first came to me, it was through another sacred helper. Eagle took me in her talons, and she flew underneath the sacred land. Swift and sure, her wings glided from the South of Mi'kma'ki up through the Earth World into the North and all the way under the waters.

We flew through the earth up to northern Newfoundland where her wings pushed higher. From out of the ground we flew in a wide arc, high into the Skyworld. Then flying back to the South, Eagle Medicine brought me home to the place where the Acadia First Nation lives.

During these three Spring Moons we can grow spiritually, emotionally, and socially by discovering and acknowledging who we are. In our sacred and cultural ways we can help ourselves and others. These ways are ancient and modern, always available to us. They include ceremony, thoughtful actions, deep and abiding feelings, and showing respect for our bodies.

We too are Sacred Medicines. When we learn the Medicine Circle, we learn to heal our bodies and minds. We become Medicines over time. Some people will become the Sacred Pipe. Not through their choice, not really. Only because others see and know who they are. What they do. How they live. If anyone claims to know, they still have a long way to go.

We can use the sacred teachings as sources of strength for our healing. In our everyday lives, we can intentionally choose to learn and heal our lives.

In our dreams, feelings, intuitions, reactions, and other emotional responses we have very powerful teachers. Listen to these parts of you, and you will know the power of these moons to help you discover new parts of yourself. By acknowledging your weaknesses and strengths, and by choosing to live an honourable way, you give the Child within you new life and guidance.

Kwe. In this wigwam of the Old Ones of the People I honour Kisikui'skw Sa'qawei Paq'tism. Elder Woman Ancient Wolf. Skw enml'ga't ala'toq Kitpu Npisuney Tumaqn. She walks home carrying Eagle Pipe Medicine. I am humbled to follow her way. To learn from her.

In this sacred time, there is much to learn. In the place of Family, the Wigwam of our People, these Sacred Moons teach us about what is most valuable – our community, our tribe, our Nation. May we each walk home to our hearts and walk steady.

Reflection

Although assumed through most of this book, a Sacred Medicine is something worth explaining for those who may not understand. The idea of a medicine has many meanings. The obvious meaning is that many things in nature have a natural medicinal purpose. They can be used to heal illness and disease. In the western way of thinking, a medicine has a purpose because it is used in healing. The material worth or value of a medicine is how it is used as such. Otherwise, it has no intrinsic social value. Not so with Mi'kmaw Medicine Traditions.

Sacred Teachings

In First Nation approaches, every plant, animal, stone and everything in the natural world has a Sacred Medicine Value. This inherent Value does not come from human beings. We do not have the power and authority to command all of creation. No. This is a subversion of our Original Intention within Creation.

Our Original Intention is to be Sacred Custodians, Carers of the Land and Sea. We are meant to be Guides, Protectors, and to Nurture the Land like our kin. But with humanity and humility. No one is perfect. And we make mistakes.

When you get your head and heart around the real meaning of these Teachings, you begin to wonder. What is a Medicine in the First Nations sense? What is Sacred about these Medicines? Why are the Teachings also called Medicines? How can a Sacred Pipe be called a Medicine, just as much as Sage, Cedar, Sweet Grass, Tobacco, and Maple Syrup? And how is this Moon time Sacred?

A blade of grass is a Sacred Medicine. That blade of grass has a purpose within Creation. Any one small wonder can tip the balance of the Worlds and bring about greater wellness or greater disorientation.

Part of the mystery comes good when you consider the heartfelt feeling of 'sacred' and come to terms with the awesome value of all things in nature simply because they exist. Not because we give them value. Children with good heart often understand this Teaching right away. They look at a butterfly, dragonfly, wasp, and a rattle snake and see all as equally beautiful and full of wonder. They may also have a different sort of respect for each, given the nature of each Spirit. But they see all as having value, beauty and wonder.

Now the notion of Medicine is similar. In the Native Way, all Medicines are Spiritual. This is hard for modern secular people to get. Very hard indeed. But reality is, the Native culture honours the spiritual. Sorry. Such is life. But to understand what this means; you might only get a few steps into the meaning before you are pulled up by your bias and prejudice. Your beliefs and values may stand in the way of understanding Native culture.

In any case, yes Medicine has its own value as part of Creation. Given to existence. Manifestation of the Divine within all of Life. Source of Energy. Energy of change, evolution, development. Part of the lifecycles and seasons of our Sacred Planet. She is also Alive and Living. We call her Mother Earth for this very reason. The Gaia theory is nothing new to Native People. We are amused when European-descent people wake up and think they have invented a theory or approach that has always existed among our Nations.

Medicines are not simply a physical or material element within Creation, they also embody Energy. We call this Energy Sacred, because this being constitutes form, unseen nature, and unrealised potential. In a sense, the Elders who walk the Medicine Path by way of herbal lore have often been able to communicate with the Spirit of Plants. These Plant Totemic Spirits come to them in dreams, visions and in subtle sensory perceptions. Before even testing the properties of a Plant Spirit, a Medicine Woman of high degree would know instinctively what the Plant is best used for and what the various purposes of the Plant Spirit may be.

This is a good illustration of how Medicine Practice is very close to, and yet distinct from, the Dreaming Practice of our Medicine Elders who Sit with the Pipe, and Guard the Sacred Doors of Vision Quest, Initiation, and Sweat Lodge. In a similar way, the Elders know intuitively the purpose of different actions when in Sacred Space, that may assist for example with healing of past hurts, opening of trauma for healing, moving of difficult memories, and restoration of a person after depression or anxiety. The Elders have a Sacred Way with loss and grief, with healing of personal problems, and with addressing various illness and disease.

In many ways current generations of Elders are seeking new understanding and reviving the tribe when it comes to these practices. I have devoted considerable time to the study and practice of natural approaches to health and wellness over the years. Over this time I have given careful thought to the ways that Native Medicine Practice can move forward in today's world. Counselling psychotherapy as a field holds many potentials for honouring the Dreaming and Medicine Practices of Aboriginal cultural traditions. Culturally grounded methods can positively influence changes in perception, increase self-awareness, and promote healing of past hurts. These insights focus in the areas of emotional and psychological healing and wellbeing, mental health and strengthening of social relationships. However, there are many pathways forward because the healing arts are many and constitute varied disciplines. For instance, I know several people who are well known for their herbal wisdom. Others are adept at treating illness with traditional Medicines and practices. Some have gifts in areas of hands-on energy work and healing, while others use various forms of intuitive insight that are nurtured within an open-minded First Nation cultural environment.

During this New Moon let us acknowledge there are hundreds of ways to live this First Nation spiritual path. There is just so much to learn. Consider for yourself where you might like to go with this knowledge, and how you may wish to expand your awareness and practice of these Teachings in future. M'sit No'koma. Ta'ho.

Joseph Randolph Bowers

May Etqoljewiku's Frog-Croaking Moon

Pjila'si ~ Welcome, come in, sit down.

During Etqoljewiku's Frog-Croaking Moon allow me to offer some Teachings on healing from trauma. Healing from past trauma involves becoming aware of ourselves. Trauma of many kinds pushes us to the edge. Extreme trauma can create emotional and psychic crisis. Chronic and long-term trauma can lead to despair. Many forms of trauma, including violence and ecological disaster challenge our core beliefs, values, and our identity can sometimes be shattered.

The history of colonisation is a story of violence and trauma. Often when a people are subject to violence, they feel powerless. Powerlessness under threat of oppression creates a chronic personal and social psychology based in trauma, fear, anxiety, and internalised anger. Anger turned inward often becomes depression and can be expressed in many forms of self-harm.

When the cycles of violence and trauma are not broken, the cycle continues. Anger leads to more internalised harm, and when acted out upon others, creates ongoing trauma.

But when the cycle of trauma is stopped, the negative spin is broken. Something new happens. Most of us allow these experiences to go unnoticed, we just feel better, and we might not know why. But I have made it a life's work to study trauma and healing, and let me tell you, healing is most certainly possible.

Healing from trauma occurs in many ways. For example, over many generations. Trans-generational trauma and healing for the Mi'kmaq goes back over five hundred years, representing fourteen generations. Witness to our strength and integrity comes through expressions of spiritual forgiveness, hospitality, and kindness offered to others after many generations of oppression.

Healing can occur over many years within one skin-time. Across a person's lifetime a slow healing process can be seen, such as in the lives of our family members who endured abuse as children.

We often carry our trauma in such a way that it comes to define our ability to survive, and marks our identity, sometimes like a terrible scar, and often like a badge of honour. Trauma over time can make us who we are, not by the violence or act of violation itself, but by our choice to not allow trauma to dominate who we are.

Trauma pushes us to the edge, and like many of the survivors of the Nazi war camps, we realise that no one has the ability to take away our Spirit. There is a part of us that no person can take away. Healing can happen in a brief period of time, and even in an instant. These moments may also go by without our being aware.

But in my study of healing, these small miracles are like the patterns by which snow falls upon the pine. They are like the systematic behaviour of the Ant People. There is a pattern that can be discerned in the ways that people heal. If we learn about this, we can encourage healing. In therapy my work creates an environment in which healing is more likely to occur. This process might give you some insight. Therapy is only one focused form of what people do in everyday life. Therapy is about taking these qualities of natural change and assisting people to move forward. I wish you every peace in your heart. Kitpu watch over you always.

Reflection

Psychotherapy for me is based in culturally grounded methods of practice. Others say my work is shamanistic in nature, meaning that they see my practices as involving traditional Aboriginal methods. Today the therapeutic world calls these approaches transpersonal, a word that means spiritual without the taboo that 'spiritual' carries. Transpersonal psychology is a distinct field of practice and theory. It could just as easily be called spiritual psychology.

Consider during this Moon how you may like to work with healing in your own life. Perhaps the issue is small, or large. Only you can determine its importance. Give the following exercise a go and see what happens for yourself.

Take a few blank pieces of paper. The size is not important. Place them in a circle, with one in front of your feet. One a few steps in front of you. Another to your left, and the last to your right. Then stand in front of the first piece, this will be 'home base.'

In home base, see, feel and listen to an issue or problem that you have. Pick something a bit easy, not too difficult. Bring up in your awareness the issue in its natural form. Gauge how it feels on a scale of one through to ten. One is easy and not very important or difficult. And ten is terrible, and extreme and awful to deal with. Remember where the issue is at when you feel it naturally. Now, look down at your feet and ask your body to leave the issue in this spot where the paper is at. You can step on the paper if you want to and leave the issue there. You can tell yourself you can come back anytime to the same feeling if and when you want to.

Now, take a step to the position to your left. Call this position two. Here look back at the issue in position one. Do you feel any differently now, looking back at the issue over there? Take note of any changes. Some people say they feel odd looking at the issue, they never did that before. Others say they feel less intense. Gauge the issue for you here - where is it at on your scale of one to ten? Now think for a moment, do you see the issue over there any differently? If so, in what way? When that is enough for you, look at your feet and ask your body to leave this experience in position two so that you can move on to the next place.

When you are ready, move to the spot next on your left. This is the one farthest away from the issue. As you step into that place, look back at position two, and home base. Now you are another step removed and further away from the original issue. Look at position two, how do you feel now? Look back at home base, how does this feel for you now? Many people say this spot feels even better because they have even less feeling for the issue than they had before. Regardless how it feels, rate yourself on the scale. Is it any different from home base, or position two?

Now look at your feet again and ask your body to leave the experience there with the paper. When you are ready, go to the fourth position, which is closer to the original issue but still, not quite there yet. People often share a reluctance to go there, because it feels like going closer to the original problem. I say, that is OK. This is a learning experience for your body and inner mind. When you go to the fourth base you can learn something helpful as well. Go to fourth base and stand there.

Look back at third position, second position, and home base each in turn. How does it feel now looking at each of these experiences? Again, check in with the intensity of the feeling and rate yourself on the scale. Compare how you felt in each position. If you could choose where to stand that feels the best, where would that be for you? Everyone has a different take on this, so follow your own feeling.

In fourth position close your eyes and imagine all that you have learned coming into your body and mind in fullness. As if all these experiences were rolled up into one, all the resources given to you now in position four. When you are ready, stand in the middle of the circle and pull in all the experiences into your body. Allow this a few deep breaths, until you feel everything coming together, take one last deep breath and let it go.

Now, look around the circle. You can go back to home base now and see if it feels the same. Most people say no, it feels different. They often say they will never feel the same way again about the issue, it is just changed. Others say, yeah, they can access the same feelings, but they nearly have to choose to go there, like it does not come naturally anymore. Others say they can feel the same way, because it was just so difficult or powerful already and they can access it just the same. But part of them has changed. Maybe how they carry that burden has shifted in some way they don't understand.

You can now walk around the circle and collect all the papers into one. As you do this, call into yourself all the learning, wisdom, and experience that came through the exercise into your body, heart and mind. You have just engaged a form of contemporary therapeutic practice that honours the wisdom and basic principles of Sacred Ceremony. This process can be taken up in the forest or field, under the stars, or by the Sacred Fire. You have engaged the Medicine Practice of our Elders to work with an issue from different places in the Sacred Circle. M'sit No'koma. Ta'ho.

Joseph Randolph Bowers

June Nipniku's Summer Moon

Pjila'si ~ Welcome, come in, sit down.

Nipniku's Summer Moon is the beginning of a new moon cycle celebrating the power and creativity of Youth. These three moons are all about the Youth in us. Take time to build up your Youth. They are future leaders, healers, teachers, and parents. They deserve and need our respect.

The Sacred Cardinal Direction of these moons is South. The Sacred Colour is Red, for the fiery energy of the Sun that we find in Youth. The Sacred Element is Fire, and Time of Day is toward Noon. The Sacred Herb is Cedar, a very pure and potent herb with powerful astringent, cleansing, enduring, and preservative qualities. The Sacred Helper is the Wolf People. Paq'tism goes ahead of the tribe to see if the way is clear. In broad daylight the Wolf People might take some rest under shade. We learn to pace ourselves during our Youth. Paq'tism is fiercely loyal to the pack, and during our Youth our loyalty is often tested under fire.

It is no coincidence that during June we celebrate Father's Day in Canada. The role that fathers play in guiding the energy of Youth is vital and cannot be underestimated. During these summer moons ahead we need to affirm the importance of Youth and Fathers in our lives. Affirmation and disclosure are the key life challenges of Youth. During our Youth we realise many things about ourselves and others. To be affirmed is essential for self-esteem and self-worth to grow. Fathers, you must learn to affirm your Youth. One kind word can last a lifetime. One harsh word can crush a spirit. Take care in your words and deeds.

As a Youth grows in self-awareness, they need to feel safe in disclosing their ideas to others. If they feel judged, they might retreat into a shell. They may hide in music, parties or substance abuse. When Youth feel isolated, all kinds of trouble can occur for them. Maintaining strong and enduring relationships is crucial during these years of intense growth and change. Disclosing your part of the story is really important. This can assist them in understanding their limitations and strengths.

Spiritually, there is a Youth in everyone us. Our inner Youth calls us to explore, take risks, and like the Alpha Paq'tism track the territory ahead to see what there is to learn. The energy of Youth is at the heart of political organisation where people band together for a common cause. Youth are passionate to learn and discover who they are. They value tradition just as much as they wish to create new pathways. Youth symbolize for the Mi'kmaq a powerful celebration and upholding of culture and values. During Youth we learn our language, traditions, and lifeways. Or we reject these and set off on a different path.

Youth is a time of many important decisions that often impact twenty, forty or sixty years down the road. We older folks know this, because we have been there, done that.

Youth please take a moment to listen to your Elders and yes, listen to your parents. They have been around the block a few times. If you learn respect for them, you build a solid foundation for everything else in life. By respecting your parents and Elders, you learn to respect yourself. You will gain the best secret that most people never get. Respect is the first step to a powerful life.

Reflection

During this New Moon take a moment to get to know the Youth in your life. Is this your child, another's child, or youth in your world? Or is this your inner Youth? Pledge to give this Youth the time of day, and to spend time with them now and in future. Make plans and keep them. Youth need something dependable. You need to be dependable, for yourself, your inner Youth, and the Youth in your life. M'sit No'koma. Ta'ho.

Sacred Teachings

Nipk/Summer Moons

July Peskewiku's Feather-shedding Moon

Pjila'si ~ Welcome, come in, sit down.

Do you ever feel lost? Emm... There was once a young boy who liked to wander in the woods towards the end of day. One day when the sun was high, he wandered off down the trail he knew well. Something caught his eye. He left the trail without any trace.

His dad used to tell him, 'If you go into the woods, mark your trail, so you can trace your steps.' Little No Fear did not listen. He walked off the trail. He disappeared in the bush without a trace.

When he turned around, he realised the day was passing. Brother Sun was low in Sky World. Shadows hung heavy. Moss and brush were thick now. Wet damp forest lay all around Little No Fear. Suddenly, he felt a pain stab his heart. His breath got short. What is this? He thought.

Frantically he found himself breaking a twig here and there, marking the branches as he walked. Then with quick steps, he could not run because the brush was too thick. He raced in his mind, what will I do? Sun is going down. What did Dad tell me? He heard the words ringing in his ears like the snap of a belt across his back side, 'Mark your trail, mark your trail...'

He started to sweat from his forehead, his palms all wet now, his shirt soaked. His breath got fast and short, and suddenly Little No Fear realised he was hyperventilating. Then all of a sudden, wham! He realised he was afraid!

This made him stop. He fell to his knees in the mossy forest and pulled his arms around his legs. He took slow, deep breaths. He said to himself, OK. I've messed up now. But pull it together. I am not lost. I am exploring. Now. Slowly. How will I get myself out of this one?

Judging from the shadows he knew he had one hour before it was completely dark. He had been going in circles for some time. He had nothing to make fire. It would be a very cold and damp night. He resigned himself to find shelter by brush or stone and settle. Then a thought occurred to him.

He remembered a logged section of forest was not far away. Then he thought, there must be logging trails. Then he did the best he could to walk toward the South where he thought the logged area to be. From thick bush where he couldn't see more than five feet ahead suddenly, he was in a clearing. With just enough light at dusk, he found a trail that led where, he didn't know. But at least the ground was dry.

From out of nowhere he saw a power line! He then realised he had walked across forty acres of thick brush that day, from one end of the forest to the other, getting lost and going in circles throughout the middle of the area. Now he knew his bearings and walked back North to his four-wheeler where he quickly changed out of his soaked clothing and put on the extra duds that he kept for after a swim in the river. As he was wiping himself with a towel and putting on fresh clothes, he prayed. He felt a deep respect for his father's advice. He resolved to never go into the forest out of mere curiosity. He found his Medicine Pouch and walking back to the edge of the thick brush, he said a prayer.

'Grandfathers of this land, thank you for protecting me today. Not from the forest. Wela'lia, for protecting me from myself. It was not wise what I did.' In humility he gave a large handful of Tobacco to the Spirits of his Grandfathers, to Spirits of the Forest. That night Little No Fear drove away from the forest with a lot of healthy respect in his heart.

Reflection

What do you fear the most? Have a little talk with your fear. Imagine it as a person or thing sitting in front of you. Have a talk. See what this fear wants to give you. Ask. What do you want for me, fear? You may just be a bit surprised what comes up for you. M'sit No'koma. Ta'ho.

Joseph Randolph Bowers

August Kisikwekewiku's Fruit and Berry-ripening Moon

Pjila'si ~ Welcome, come in, sit down.

When the fruits and berries ripen and the moon is full, Kisikwekewiku tells us our youth will turn into young adults and things will change forever.
Relationships reach a new level, and desires for love and family grow strong. New families come to be where there was only potential. And the reality of daily life moves on with new adult responsibilities.
Who would have known each moon of the year has so many teachings for us? But they do, each one in turn.

In the Southern Door the sun reaches its zenith during this moon, and the year begins slowly to wane towards the winter moons once again. Fond memories for me from my youth are of the third week of August when the air subtly changes. Funny enough a similar turning time occurs in the Southern hemisphere on the opposite side of the planet from Mi'kma'ki.

In our Sacred Land you can see the Golden Eagle flying in the Southern Door. Paq'tism goes ahead. In Australia the Great Wedgetail Eagle rides the skies. This Eagle became part of my Dreaming and Medicine Path over the years. And I have learned these Ways with even more humility.

At one meet up, I found myself sharing the story of our Mi'kmaq Elder's Teachings about how to care for the Sacred Eagle Feather. How we dress the Feather Elder with care, honour and colour, and how we keep it safe to preserve, protect and keep its Energy strong. How we burn Sacred Herbs to cleanse ourselves before touching the Sacred Spirit Feather... And how we handle this Medicine with respect...

A person in the group stood closer and closer to me. I felt their Spirit growing strong again with pride. During a simple ceremony of thanksgiving, I held the Sacred Wedgetail Feather and prayed. Passed that Feather Elder around the Circle. Sang a song of Honour.

When the Feather Elder reached this person's hands they could not easily let go. I knew that Feather Elder found a place. One of the other Aboriginal Elders caught my eye, and we looked at this person. We knew. Sometimes things just happen, and you know. You just know.

Later on, that person stood up at the meeting. They said through tear filled eyes that they wanted to honour the Mi'kmaq Nation. They wanted to honour our Elders for their teaching on caring for the Sacred Medicines because this gave them back their Dreaming. They said that people from their community had talked and agreed to work with the youth in their community to carve a Sacred Container from one of their Sacred Trees, and to carve symbols of their Dreaming into that box. They said that the Living Tree would be used to protect the Sacred Wedgetail Dreaming of their Nation. They said this was the first time their Dreaming had been awakened since before the times of the massacres that destroyed their way of life.

That Sacred Eagle Feather Elder taught us many lessons that day. Those in that room pledged to care for the Feather Elder. The tribe who made the Sacred Box would pass that Feather Elder from tribe to tribe, to share the healing and the story of how to care for this Feather Elder so to restore the Dreaming in a part of Australia most hit by invasion.

When praying with Elder Medicine the land sings to us… In the fullness of youth our passionate hearts hear her voice. We listen. We sing. We dance.

Mothers and fathers, love your youth this month and teach them even one new word of our language, teach them to know respect. Teach them how to love. Honour them for hearing the cries of our Earth Mother. Honour them for their purity of heart, as they will need courage in the moons ahead.

Reflection

As you cycle through the seasons and come to respect the First Nation Moons you might begin to realise how many lessons there are to learn in life. Living in a balanced and sacred manner is an art form you get to perfect your whole life through. No ending to this journey.

In this New Moon allow the darkness to seep into your heart and realise that this too is the Life of Spirit, the Essence of Evolution, the Power of Being. Ask this Energy of Life to pour into your heart and mind, and to bring peace and deeper understanding.

Remember the Eagle who rises highest toward Creator, who rides the Sky World with confidence. We could only be so blessed. We human beings will always have such limited scope in our vision and in our ability to comprehend the nature of the world.

Give thanks for all you have learned. Thankful hearts are the primary purpose of our existence. Thankfulness opens many doors, pathways and passages. Try it out and discover for yourself the Power in Thanksgiving. M'sit No'koma. Ta'ho.

Joseph Randolph Bowers

September Wikumkewiku's Moose-calling Moon

Pjila'si ~ Welcome, come in, sit down.

Wikumkewiku's Moose-calling Moon marks new rhythms of the Western Door entering the sacred circle of life.

During the next three moons the life stage is Adult. The Sacred Colour is Black like the shadows that fall during the late afternoon. The Sacred Element is Air, which grows crisper and sharper, and during adult life our minds can become clearer if we take up our path and walk in a good way.

The Sacred Elder tells me Muin Nation, Bear Nation guards the Western Door. Twin Brown Bear Woman and her family of cubs we honour during these moons. A powerful Spirit of Protection covers the Mi'kmaq Nation at this time. Ta'ho.

The Sacred Herb of these moons is Sage. Sage helps us when we are adults because our minds easily become confused. Spirits hang on to us. Sage releases these spirits and cleanses our thoughts. Our bodies need this smoke. As a psychotherapist this makes sense because the simple ceremony of cleansing each day creates positive and resourceful thoughts. This is very healthy. It is important to acknowledge we are a part of a larger world, an ecosystem, an environment. By cleansing with smoke we humble ourselves. This teaches us many values essential to being Mi'kmaw, to being human.

The Sacred Places of these moons are the World Beneath the Water and World Beneath the Earth. During these moons Kitpu flies through the Underworlds to bring strength and power to sustain us during the winter moons ahead.

The Adult Moons are a very special time in the family life cycle. We bring new life into the world and become parents physically and, if we are wise, also spiritually. We put much energy into making a living and paying the bills. Our children take up our lives and focus of energy. At the same time, the undercurrents of our identity are growing steady every day and night.

For these reasons, many adults rely on the Medicine People for advice during a time in their lives when they are too busy to listen spiritually. But we all have this capacity to sit with the Medicines, and to become the Medicine in our own lives.

These Sacred Moons of autumn are given to us adults to help us remember who we are called to be. The Worlds Below and the Shadow Times of these Moons tell us that our lives will not continue forever. We are mortal. We will go back to the Earth and become Dust with our Ancestors.

We are reminded to just stop. Now and then. Even only for five minutes. Even only for a few seconds. Life is never too busy to say thank you. To look around. Stomp on the earth. To feel alive. Celebrate all our hard work. Get off our back sides. Get moving with a new project. To keep hope alive for our children and their children who will come, surely as the sun rises.

These are just a few of the Sacred Rhythms that make our People unique and distinct, and that also unite us with all of humanity. These seasons of life are the Medicine of our Dreaming.

If you listen carefully, and place your ear to the ground, you will surely hear the heartbeat of your Ancestor calling out to you. Dancing around a large fire. Dancing under the stars of the Bear Nation. Singing the Song of the Stars.

No one else will hear what only you can hear. This is your day. Brother, sister, don't throw it away with booze and gambling. Don't be short sighted when you are really gifted and talented. The world will not change. Only you can change what you can change with Creator's help. This is the secret of life. Grab hold and be free.

Reflection

You might want to begin your review for this year sometime during this or the next New and Growing Moon. This review will bring you back three years to the beginning of this book and your process of learning and growing in these First Nation Ways. You may want to decide how much time to devote to that review, as you may need to set aside a few weekends here or there. Or a series of early mornings, or a quiet time at night.

What Medicines are important in your life now? What have you learned of the Sacred Ways of the Elders? What parts of yourself do you value the most? What issues have you faced, or new issues you might want to work with in the Sacred Circle?

What are your next projects in life? Where do you see yourself in a year or five years' time? How would you like to be, in your skin?

Remember to embody your new life in actions of kindness. Recall that you too are a Sacred Medicine. Treat yourself with kindness. M'sit No'koma. Ta'ho.

Joseph Randolph Bowers

Toqa'q/Autumn Moons

October Wikewiku's Animal-fattening Moon

Pjila'si ~ Welcome, come in, sit down.

This time of year gives a way to communicate, to see and express beauty, and to feel the fire of justice and truth. Communication gives people a way to make connections between the worlds. The ancient and modern, the forest and city, the sky and underworld, the way of giving and receiving.

Seeing and expressing beauty is basic to humanity. We need beauty and ways to transform sorrow into joy. As spirits we are oriented towards healing even after eons of suffering.

Justice and truth might come slower for those born this time of year. But look out, when they are ready to stand their ground no one will be able to move them from what they have pondered for a long time.

This moon shifts the tides into the Western Door in powerful ways, and in the West, we begin to desire Elder wisdom. We are old enough as adults to realise how little we know, and how much there is to learn in life. We start growing a little humility that slowly replaces the 'know it all' days of our youth.

As the weather shifts this moon, so our spirits open up to new insight. We instinctively start preparing for the winter ahead. Our psyche and heart feel contrary to this push to survive, with a melancholy that naturally comes with the lengthening evenings and shorter days. In my way, this moon is filled with different energies and new projects that arise. It is a natural time to think about mental health, personal and family wellbeing, spiritual ceremony and healing.

While the harvest might allow a fattening of body to store away energy for the winter to come, still many of our people are enduring great suffering and injustice living in Fourth World conditions in first class countries. The trans-generational trauma we carry from the residential school times and from chronic racism and threats of violence over many generations have made us stronger as a people. Our spiritual teachings grow even today. Our Ancestors come to us in our dreams, dance, and song. And we each are given a song to sing by our Ancient guardians who watch over us.

For me the Medicine calling came during my childhood, sitting on the track, waiting quietly for the wild Deer People to come along. Later on a young Mi'kmaw boy moved in next door. He told me to always mark my way when exploring the forest. He taught me about tracking, how to listen to the hidden song of the birds, how to watch their flight, and how to appreciate patience and humility. Several moons later he was taken away to yet another foster home. Before he left, he gave me his tomahawk and said, 'With this, mark your way in the forest. Now you will never get lost. Remember these words my brother.' There is so much we will never know about the world. The world is a very mysterious place.

I don't know any more why this life for me is a spiral that brings me back to where I began in my Youth. Why my Spirit has to come home to the woods of Mi'kma'ki where my Ancestors from all Nations found a home, where we were joined into one family under God through the sacred vows of marriage. But the thing is, we may never know why. 'Why' is not our song to sing. 'Why' leads us down the wrong path.

We need to ask, 'How can I listen? How can I honour? How can I love? How can I take up this path Creator has for me?' Then life will open up.

Reflection

During this New Moon ask yourself different questions. I found that when I ask why, the answers never come. But when I ask how, there are new possibilities that open up. Sure. It is harder doing it this way. If I ask how, and I get ideas of what I can do, then I have to be responsible.

In ways, it is easier to be defeated than to move on. Easier to stay stuck than to take responsibility. Easier to blame other people than take up my path and walk for myself.

But you have come this far. Are you going to give up now? I don't think so. I think you are amazing. I believe you are full of wonder and light and power. I see you in my vision, clear as day, you have become one of the Sacred Stars in the Night Sky. During this New Moon I see you. And you are called to live this Path of the Sacred Warrior. You are called to become a Being of the Light. M'sit No'koma. Ta'ho.

November Keptekewiku's River-freezing Moon

Pjila'si ~ Welcome, come in, sit down.

Indigenous peoples have very strong ethical and legal boundaries based in traditional culture. These ways are wholistic. They honour the ecology of all life and sustain the environment around us.

Many Indigenous peoples around the world are developing very strong ethical codes of practice for health care, mental health services, counselling, and psychotherapy. They are creating ways of honouring Traditional Medicine Teachings that encourage traditional practitioners to work alongside mainstream health workers including medical doctors.

During Keptekewiku's River-freezing Moon, I honour the traditional Keepers of Medicines. I honour their gifts of insight, vision, and healing. I honour the Ancient Ones who first greeted the flouting islands over five hundred years ago.

We today cannot carry the Full Power of the Ancient Medicines. We are not strong enough. We do not have the strength of our Ancestors.

In great humility, we can Allow the Medicines to Carry Us. We must not claim to be anything. This is a life-long path of learning. In actions do what is right.

The Medicine Path is a long and difficult walk. This commitment is life-long, and we face many unknowns. We walk in trust within a living planetary system that protects us even when we make mistakes. Creator is very loving and compassionate. Mother Earth's sense of justice is harsh at times, but ultimately brings transformation for our lives.

The Mi'kmaq need a strong code of ethics for health care and allied health practices. It is not my place to step in and do this work. A ground swell in the community is needed. A cultural revival and spiritual fire in the heart of our Nation will open new doors.

The Medicine Keepers will be invited to places of honour once again, and they will stand with the politicians and dignitaries. I have seen this, and it will come to pass. The Medicine Councils of Elders will be acknowledged in new ways. One day soon a Mi'kmaq Code of Practice will govern not only Traditional Medicine practices but will also inform mainstream approaches.

Traditional Healers and Keepers of Sacred Medicine and Dreaming will engage in their practices of culture and spiritual work alongside nurses, doctors, counsellors, psychologists, and allied professionals. This is already happening in other Indigenous Nations. Mainstream health systems around the world are coming to appreciate, honour, and respect Traditional Medicine.

For over two decades I have worked in the allied health sector in Australia as a practitioner and a scholar and am happy to say that my approach to these issues has been highly regarded. I have very strongly critiqued mainstream health care and challenged fields of counselling and psychology to move beyond colonial and oppressive models of Euro-American philosophy based in racism, bias, and prejudice. These beliefs and values underpin the whole health care sector and form the theories that support mainstream practice. This must change.

To move beyond these ways means creating post-colonial models of theory and practice. To do this, we Indigenous people must walk the talk and get with the program. We are the ones today who are asked to change the way things are done, so our children will live with pride in who they are. New Medicine Keepers are ready to come to our Nation. Will we welcome the Seventh Generation? Mi'kmaq Nation awaken to the power within You. Eagle Medicine sends up healing smoke.

Reflection

What are your Medicine Ways unique to your own life? Simple though they may be, you are called to honour, carry and protect certain Medicine and Dreaming traditions. Perhaps these are personal to you.

Remember that in the Mi'kmaw Way, there are different levels of service. The first is always personal. There is a Personal Sacred Pipe, for this very purpose. Every individual has their own Way in Life. They need to find, nurture and protect their own Being, such that they remain strong and able to assist other people when necessary. They can be strong, without being too much of a burden to others, and find their path in life.

Then there is a family level of service. For this reason, someone in the family may be asked or called to carry the Sacred Family Pipe. Usually this falls to the Mother or Father of the family, but often I have seen this duty arising in one of the youth of the family. This happening challenges the whole family to respect each other in new ways, which is good to see. Youth can also carry the Family Pipe in ways that require openness, creativity, and humility by the parents. They are often challenged to listen when normally they might not.

Next there is a community level of service. A Community Sacred Pipe is a very demanding task to carry. The person who is asked or called to do this service must be open to the nature of the spiritual and temporal work that needs doing. Often this person may be burdened with the cares of the community, for clean water, access to food, dealing with homes that are not adequate through the long winter, coping with family upset and breakdown, and feeling the weight of issues of substance abuse, family violence and sickness and disease. All of these issues are part of the life of the Native community, and by extension, the community of human beings. Carrying the Sacred Community Pipe includes all of these responsibilities and more.

Next there is a Nation Pipe. This level of service takes in all of the rest and includes the national wellbeing of the People, the Tribe as a Nation. This level of responsibility includes the political, social and economic wellbeing of the many communities who make up the Nation. Pipe Carriers who have carried the Nation Pipe have a very demanding job. Some become very active members of the political and social life of the People. Others become solitaries and spend their lives in prayer, and the leaders of the communities and Nation are wise to visit these persons or to consult with them in humility regarding the many issues facing the Nation.

These levels of service reveal only a few of the different pathways that exist and that can teach us. This reminds us that everyone plays a part. Very few end up Carrying the Nation Pipe of the People. But everyone can and may be called to Carry a Personal Pipe as a Way of Prayer and Ceremonial Practice that grounds, gives balance, and opens the Sacred Doors of personal growth and development. Each person has an important part to play.

I pray you are empowered with this knowledge and that you will seek the Sacred Pathways for your life. I pray these open up for you. And give you deep inner vision. Much beauty and contentment. And an overflowing energy of joy and happiness. M'sit No'koma. Ta'ho.

Joseph Randolph Bowers

December Kjiku's The Great Moon

Pjila'si ~ Welcome, come in, sit down.

Kjiku's The Great Moon marks a completion of the Sacred Medicine Wheel of the year. The next three moons rest in the Northern Door. The Sacred Colour is White.

White Ochre is painted on our bodies during the mourning cries. White represents the Great Spirit, the purity of childhood, and the snows that bring a stillness and quiet to the forest floor. White brings us back to the purity of water, the water of our initiation in Mother's womb. White is the sacred essence of all colours that brings earth, air, fire and water into one symbol of new life and hope.

The Sacred Element of these moons is Water. Because these Moons Honour our Elders, water represents wisdom, love, and service. An Elder Tree makes room for other creatures to live. Water falls from the highest places and seeks the lowest place, just in order to serve all Nations of Mother Earth. We can learn so much from the Water Nation. No surprise that many Sacred Water Ceremonies are based in Woman's Medicine. Through water we are given new birth, cleansing, and renewal.

The Sacred Herb of these moons is Tobacco. A most humble and noble herb, Tobacco Nation was never meant to be taken like an addictive drug. For years I smoked without a sacred purpose, and always felt the need to have tobacco near my body. Only in later years I realised the spiritual teachings around Tobacco. OK. I am a slow learner! When these teachings came to me, I was freed of my addiction.

My new discipline was to put Tobacco into my Medicine Pouch that I wore around my neck. When I felt like smoking, instead I offered a pinch of this Helper as a prayer and a personal sacrifice. I gave my addition to the Sacred Helper. Every time I craved a smoke, I offered up a prayer instead. This new practice gave me a spiritual purpose that replaced my addiction. It wasn't easy! But this basic challenge told me that unless I changed my beliefs and values toward the Tobacco Nation, I would never respect my body or any other teachings in life. Just think about this.

This was years ago. It was one of my first challenges. Smoke like any other person unaware or become conscious and make Tobacco a Sacred Offering. I chose to go the Red Road. That was before any new growth or understanding or any of the Sacred Teachings came my way. I had nothing to go on. Just my feeling that this was the right thing to do. This one choice changed my life.

When you realise your body craves healing and right relationships, you start to change your attitude. What came to me first as a twisted addiction to 'old tobaccee' transformed into a respect for traditional forms of respect. By coming back to our teachings, we have a very clear path to health and being more fully alive.

Reflection

These Moons inspire us to take our journey seriously. Time is precious. How will you live today like it was your only moment to exist? Slow and steady we are changing our circumstances and growing through these challenges. The Sacred Helpers of the Mi'kmaq Nation Medicine People during these Moons are the Migjigi Nation, the Turtle People. Not surprising that during these Moons Turtle People seek the protection of mud and the deep waters under the ice of the lake. They seek a place at the Heart of Mother Earth. Their Elder wisdom and ancient knowledge make them a Powerful People, and they have many teachings for those patient enough and humble enough to listen.

You have been one of these spirits willing to listen and learn. Over these past three years you have taken a path of personal growth and reflection. In many ways, this process is like a social and spiritual initiation into the mysteries of Native spiritual practice.

Congratulations on getting to this place. This now is a very special time. Allow yourself to reflect on the pathwork undertaken. Recall the times you have sat during the dark moon tide. Remember the many full moons and how you chose to celebrate, contemplate and open your heart and life to new levels of awareness.

What new relationships have opened up for you during these times? Honour these now. Give thanks in your heart and offer Sacred Tobacco to Mother Earth for her provisions. Creator admires people who give thanks for all things, in what we see as good or bad, easy or difficult, in health or sickness, and in riches or poverty. We bring our lives as they are now to God. And Great Spirit honours our honesty, humility, and humanity.

Remember again our Native Elders, and please consider supporting them in whatever ways you can. Bring into your life more awareness of the social, historical and political issues facing First Nation communities in today's world. And don't be afraid to speak up, educate others, and share information that may change people's attitudes and beliefs.

How has your pathwork connected the personal and political? The spiritual and the ecological? The mystical and prayerful with the everyday responsibilities of your life? What vision has Creator given to you for making change in the world? My prayer for you is that you will feel deeply empowered to move mountains with your well-grounded intentions and through your practical wisdom you will open many doors. M'sit No'koma. Ta'ho.

Joseph Randolph Bowers

Postscript 2013

The tides of the seasons mean so much in Mi'kmaw and in the Native cosmologies of Aboriginal peoples around the world. We today can easily forget the thousands of ways we are dependent on nature to provide the delicate balance needed to sustain human life. At one time in the not so distant past, we lived much closer to the pulse of nature.

We can easily forget, for example, how the oceans are the first Mother of all lands. Only one or two degrees of change in the seasonal temperature of the oceans can bring disaster for weather patterns around the globe. As the earth warms, we see the results of climate change all around us.

In my tribal country I have taken note of many changes. No longer is there a steady snow like there was in my childhood. Only twenty-five or thirty-five years have passed since the deep snows of the 1960s and early 1970s. Now the winters tend to bring rain in the Acadia First Nation territory, or what we call the Southern Shore. Deep snows do come, but they are rarer.

These changes bring slightly longer summers, with less annual rainfall. The clouds tend to hang in the sky and rain does not fall like it used to. The forests are also changing. Acid rain is commonly accepted these days. No longer do people even imagine of drinking fresh rainwater collected in buckets or from the roof top. No longer do many people even trust the water that flows in remote streams in the woods, or water from lakes. Whereas in my childhood we freely drank and enjoyed many streams and freshwater holes in bogs and other places in the forest.

We remember fondly licking the water from leaves as a child. Standing under a great tree and allowing the rain to fall upon the branches, and holding my lips open to the water falling from the sky. It was common for us to drink the water collected by a Lady Slipper flower, a most precious and now endangered species. We did not pick them but lay on the wet shrubs of the bog lands and gently bending the flower over, drinking the water of the Creator in such a way that it was like a form of worship.

Then sitting upon a deer trail and waiting for many hours. They did come. And watched me silently from a distance. We imagine sharing many stories and teachings then, while our eyes watched each other through the trees.

A simplicity of life guarded the Sacred Doors of the World. During those days, a magic seemed to live in the forest. Perhaps children today can feel that same magic, I do not know. All I can say is that my heart still believes in the Sacred Worlds of our Ancestors and of our People. We have endured so much, all of us, of all Nations. We have survived and today we still face many enormous challenges that are in fact just as difficult than any our foremothers and forefathers ever faced.

Not only do we have to manage our daily lives, feeding and caring for our families, but we have local, regional, provincial, state level, and national politics to contend with. We are influenced by global trends, economics, policies and corporate practices that reach far beyond practical or common-sense knowledge. It takes years of formal learning to cope with the basics in today's world.

The same can be said for Traditional Ways. It takes time to learn cultural and spiritual teachings. It requires dedication to learn the ways of local ecosystems and how our lives are governed and influenced by the tides of the seasons. It was this last insight that led me on the path of reconnection with Mi'kmaw cultural heritage. I had by that time already studied in the western academe for the better part of twenty-four years, if you include twelve years of grade school. Even then I worked in the academe for another fifteen years before moving into other fields of practice, but still keeping a foot in that world as an Adjunct Senior Lecturer.

After travelling the western path to its natural conclusions, we yearn for what any western person would seek in a post-colonial era. Connection, feeling, purpose and dignity. The four qualities of life denied by the modern materialistic western canon.

In today's world people are bred to not care, and to look out for number one above all else. In the academe today people have grown cold of heart because their heads are filled with useless knowledge while their hearts are malnourished. Knowledge has always been equally life-giving and a temptation. All at once a golden key and a knife that cuts deep. Without a greater degree of humility, knowledge becomes a quest for power, influence and control.

It was essentially this path that led me here. To realise that knowledge had given me as much of what was to be had. What was missing was a cultural and spiritual connection with people in community. What was absent were times of sharing stories and being a part of people's everyday worlds. What seemed distant was a sense of the purposefulness of being a part of helping others on a daily basis. And from helping others and doing projects that made a difference gaining a sense of personal dignity.

But like many people, travelling the path of western status in learning and roles given by today's society felt like a necessary evil during those years. Those roles were important in their own right. And the parts we play today within various respected academes, with colleagues near and far, and within various communities around the world are also important and necessary pieces of work. Keeping the balance is important.

Therefore, after much living and reflection, both ways are necessary in today's world. The path of living and engaging in traditional knowledge and in Sacred Ceremonial learning is just as important as learning in schools and universities, and just as vital as taking on Indigenous scholarship and practice. Many of us may come at these paths from different directions, but ultimately if we are wise, we may end up in a very similar place. By respecting both ways of knowing we are building a much stronger society and community.

Here again, today's world is much more demanding. No longer can we be content with staying in our local communities. My life is only one small example. In my twenties I travelled across Canada and into the USA, Europe, and the Middle East. In my thirties I moved to Australia. In my forties I moved back to Canada, and then again back to Australia. These travels changed my life and gave me a much broader view of the world. Because my work and life called me to write for the Seventh Generation, nothing that I have done has been lost. While I made many sacrifices and have deeply grieved my decisions to leave my Native Land, at the end of the day I have had to surrender that grief and loss to Creator because my life was bought and paid for long before I entered this skin-time.

When we are on our path, we will realise one way or other that life always asks us to maintain steadiness, calm, assurance, and determination. These basic mature qualities of being demand that we keep our integrity, our basic decisions become real, more than fantasy, so that other people can come to rely on us with confidence. If we are like the flower that is blown away in the wind, we are surely poetic and beautiful, to be sure. But we are not a Sacred Tree under which other beings can take shelter. The spiritual path calls people to become like the Old Growth Trees, even though we may only have a small number of years. In human time, and when living a rich and full life, a year is like a thousand seasons.

Joseph Randolph Bowers

It seems that when you have taken in the teachings and stories contained within this Book of First Nation Moons, you will have not only learned but also practiced a form of Ceremony and perhaps even Prayerfulness or Mindfulness. If you learned anything from these writings, you will have considered how you are living your life and examined your conscience more than once. You may have asked yourself some difficult questions and sat listening to the silence more than you may have before. You will have taken time out to just be, and to enjoy your being. Perhaps you learned to appreciate a form of patience and acceptance of your life and circumstances in this moment. And I would hope that you may have become more aware of the world around you, of the Sacredness of the Seasons, and of the Sacred Tides of the Moons.

As we become more aware of the simple movements of the Moon we have at least one thing upon which to rely. One small anchor in a sea of changing culture, knowledge, and experience. The Mi'kmaw traditional Moon Times have given me a sense of the Sacred woven into daily and nightly life and connected me with not only my tribal country but with an appreciation and respect for other lands and places.

In my current place of residing in Waradjuri and Anaiwan Country in Australia, I have learned much about local ecology and seasons. By observing the Moon here, I have noticed the growth and flowering of certain native plants and come to associate the times of the Moon cycles with these patterns of growth. I have witnessed the life cycles of various animals and come to honour and celebrate the Power of this Land. These experiences have deeply enriched my life. After many years here I have developed a unique calendar of my own that reminds me to celebrate the local and regional ecology, as it is too easy to be distracted and sucked into the worlds of national and global media and the cultures of consumerism and crass materialism.

One thing that seems so important to me now is that we become what we focus on. People have said that what we eat we become. This is also true. But I have seen that our focus determines much about who we become over time. If I focus on the material world, I become a material man. If I focus on academic learning and intellectual development, over time I become an intellectual man and a scholar. If my focus is on loving other people and giving of myself in a generous spirit, then over time my life will become more caring, more selfless in regard for others, and more generous of heart and time. When my attention is on plants and animals, seasons and the Moon, my spiritual life seems to grow and become more balanced and part of my everyday life. Indeed, I have found that when my focus is on the spiritual matters of life my overall experience in the world softens, becomes more diffuse, less stressful and anxious and more in touch with the moment.

For these and many other reasons it felt like a heart-focused task to share this book with you. In my own strange way, I extend to you a welcoming and healing form of energy through these words that have come to me during a time of solitude and spiritual balance. The desire of my heart for you is that your life will blossom with goodness and kindness. This may seem trite or even silly to some, however, I believe that wishing the best for others has opened up so many doors in those people's lives. Not only do I offer this form of traditional blessing, but my efforts have extended to you over two hundred pages of meaningful insights, stories, lessons and teachings that can help to guide and inspire your way.

Every gift in life is better when passed on to others. It is better to give than to receive. And in giving we in fact open up a spiritual blessing that signals to the Spirit Guides that we are ready to receive more. More comes to us when we are generous of heart.

Joseph Randolph Bowers

While I want to thank you for purchasing this book, I would also ask that you pass on this book or gift another copy of the same to your friends, family, loved ones, and most especially to your enemies and to people to whom you have had issues in the past. They may think you are just nuts or mad but giving something to them may also open up their minds and hearts in ways you may never have expected. They may even learn something. You can be assured of a very large smile and a warm chuckle knowing that they will read this little paragraph at the end of this book. The idea of karma is often quite funny. Goodness comes to all of God's children regardless whether we are good, bad, or just plain silly. We are all on this path together. A bit of humility never hurts too much, even when our pride gets the better of us. We can at least have a good laugh at ourselves and move on.

To conclude I offer this poem given to the Mi'kmaq by the Eagle Medicine Nation Pipe.

Postscript 2023

    We had felt to republish this book in previous years, but life got the better of that idea. It seemed important to bring this little book into print again this year… we are not sure why this is the case. We simply listen to the tides.

    It took us a great deal of discipline to keep our fingers away from editing the original. Given that this material was first published in the MMN News, and edited for book publication back when, the historical text makes more sense to us than making changes to reflect current perspectives. The one change we notice is that we would often replace the personal pronoun 'I' with 'we' and this itself is highly symbolic of growth toward elder wisdom.

    With that thought alone, we will close this collection and offer a few brief words in poetic prose.

    Take care, and all the best to you and yours.

Joseph Randolph Bowers

Into the solitude of the woods
Walk steady, walk sure
Into the quiet of the brook
Sit down
Into the place where Chickadee sings
Put up your hand
Feed our Friends our People
Feed them well.
Dance the beat of the Sacred Drum
Move your body with your heart
Dance the rhythm of Endless Ages
Feel the movement of Fundy Tides
Feel the flowing of the tides.
Into the solitude of the woods
Walk steady, walk sure
Into the quiet of the brook
Sit down, stay a while…

M'sit No'koma. Ta'ho.

www.ingramcontent.com/pod-product-compliance
Lightning Source LLC
Chambersburg PA
CBHW071830300426
44116CB00009B/1496